First Edition

Genuine Autographed Collectible

Do you want me to sign it in ink or in lipstick?

Gift Card

Date:

To:

From:

Message:

What Do Books Do?
BOOKS ARE POWERFUL!

Books **Educate!**
Books **Enlighten!**
Books **Empower!**
Books **Emancipate!**
Books **Entertain!**
Books **Spring** Eternal!
Books **Drive** Exploration!
Books **Spark** Evolution!
Books **Ignite** Revolution!

SHARON ESTHER LAMPERT

Gift Shop: BooksArePowerful.com

POETRY JEWELS

Diamonds
Emeralds
Sapphires
Rubies & Pearls

KADIMAH PRESS
Gifts of Genius

Literature, Poetry, Judaism, Jewish History, Creativity, Art, Genius, Sharon Esther Lampert

POETRY JEWELS: Diamonds, Emeralds, Sapphires, Rubies, and Pearls

Sharon Esther Lampert is One of the World's Greatest Poets

©2022 by Sharon Esther Lampert. All Rights Reserved.
No part of this book may be used or reproduced in any manner whatsoever without written permission except in the case of brief quotations embodied in critical articles and reviews.

KADIMAH PRESS: GIFTS OF GENIUS

Books may be purchased for education, business, or sales promotional use.

ISBN Hardcover: 978-1-885872-15-9
ISBN Paperback: 978-1-885872-16-6
ISBN E-Book: 978-1-885872-17-3
Library of Congress Catalog Card Number: 2021921291

Fan Mail:
Website: www.SharonEstherLampert.com
Email: FANS@SharonEstherLampert.com

For Global Online Orders and Distribution:
INGRAM 1 Ingram Blvd. La Vergne, TN 37086-3629
Phone: 615-793-5000, Fax orders: 615-287-6990

Age 9
THE QUEEN HAS ARRIVED!
"My daughter is a poet, philosopher, and teacher.
She is the Princess & the Pea!
BEAUTY & BRAINS!"
MOMMY
XOXO

LOVE OF MY LIFETIME: MOMMY EVE PAIKOFF LAMPERT

Book Design and Interior: Creative Genius Sharon Esther Lampert

Editor: Dave Segal

First Edition

Manufactured in the United States of America

Dedication

Hannah Szenes
My Metaphysical Sister

Born: July 17, 1921, Budapest, Hungary
Murdered: November 7, 1944, Budapest, Hungary

"**One great poem** is lucky.
Two great poems mean I have something,
but I don't know what it is.
Three great poems mean I have something,
and I have to learn to work it—but there is
no instruction manual.
Four great poems mean I have a gift,
and the gift is a mystery."
—Sharon Esther Lampert

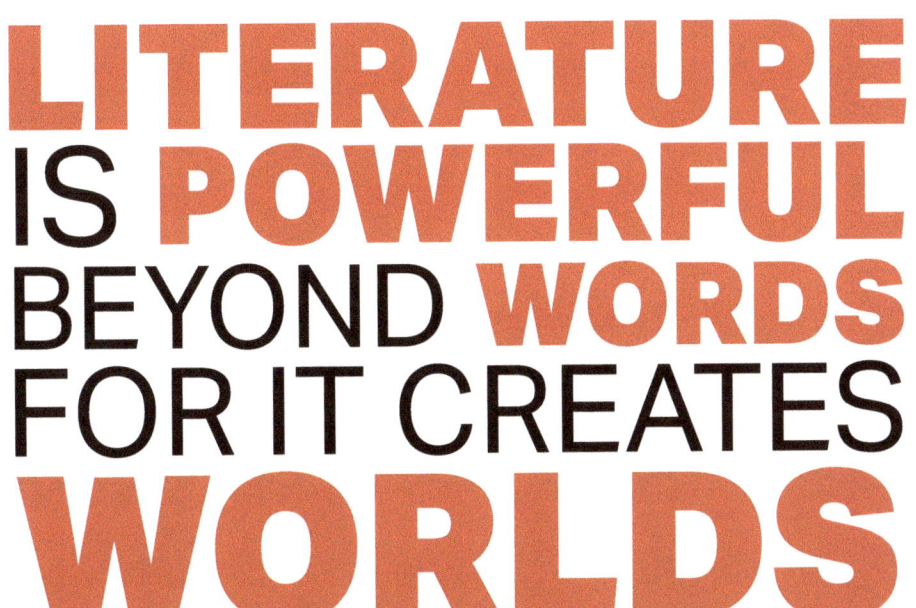

LITERATURE IS POWERFUL BEYOND WORDS FOR IT CREATES WORLDS

Sharon Esther Lampert
Poet, **P**rophet, **P**hilosopher, **P**eacemaker, **P**aladin of Education, **P**rodigy

SEE THE WORLD THROUGH THE EYES OF A CREATIVE GENIUS

EIGHTEEN POETRY BOOKS
3 Editions: Hardcover, Paperback, and E-Book

The Greatest Poems Ever Written on Extraordinary World Events

1. I Stole All the Words From The Dictionary
2. **IMMORTALITY IS MINE:** Greatest Poems Ever Written on Extraordinary World Events
3. **POETRY JEWELS: D**iamonds, **E**meralds, **S**apphires, **R**ubies, and **P**earls
4. **V.E.S.S.E.L. V**ery. **E**xtra. **S**pecial. **S**haron. **E**sther. **L**ampert.
5. Does Your Kid Read Sharon Esther Lampert?
6. Does Your Professor Teach Reason-N-Rhyme?
7. What Happens When You Dress Up Albert Einstein as Marilyn Monroe?
8. Sharon Esther Lampert: The Sexiest Creative Genius in Human History
9. **SEA IN, SEE OUT:** Childhood Poem
10. **CUPID:** Language of Love — Written in Letter **C**
11. Spiraling Downward, Upward We Stand United: 911 World Trade Center Tragedy
12. In 5 Minutes, Learn 5000 Years of Jewish History
13. Love Ever Reborn Is Love Ever Newborn
14. It's Not Easy Being a **JEWISH SEX SYMBOL** But Someone Has to Do It!
    Poems Written About Sharon Esther Lampert by Her Fans
15. **SWEET NOTHINGS:** Love Portraits in Poetry
16. Witches, Whores, Wives, and Writers — Feminist Poems
17. No **F**akes! No **F**lops! No **F**illers! No **F**at! No **F**-Bomb!
18. 7 Practice Husbands: Love Portraits in Poetry

• Buy Autographed Collectibles Online

• All Global Bookstores: USA, CAN, UK, AUS, ASIA, AFRICA, INDIA and MIDDLE EAST

Table of Contents

POPULAR POEMS
- **POETREE** ... p. 1
- **THE 22 COMMANDMENTS** ... pp. 2-3
- **TRUE LOVE** ... p. 4
- **BE ART** ... p. 4
- **WORLD PEACE EQUATION** ... p. 5

- How to Read a Poem by Sharon Esther Lampert ... p. 6
- 10 Poetry Reading Tips ... p. 25

THE GREATEST POEMS EVER WRITTEN ON EXTRAORDINARY WORLD EVENTS

JUDAISM
- My Jewish Essence and Publication ... pp. 8-9
  Illustration: Florie Freshman (There are translations in Hebrew and Yiddish)
- Israeli Day Parade Float ... p. 31

JEWISH HERO POEMS
- ISRAEL'S First Astronaut: Space Legacy of a Legend JUST HEAVEN EXISTS ... p. 10
- ISRAEL'S First Olympic Gold Medal (rhyme) ... p. 11
- Yael Matzpun: PUSSYWHIPPED(rhyme) ... p. 12
- Shalom Sergeant Shalit ... p. 13
- Simon Wiesenthal: Nazi Hunter ... p. 33

JEWISH AMERICAN POEMS
- Mayor Edward Koch (rhyme) ... p. 14
- Bess Myerson: Miss Jewish America ... p. 15

JEWISH HISTORY POEMS
- The Militant Palestinian Toddler Terrorist ... p. 16
- Carmel Forest Fires: Wherever Israelis Go, Gardens Grow ... p. 17
- Gaza Strip: Salahadin Road (rhyme) ... pp. 18-19
- EPIC: Many Jews Reclaimed God ... pp. 20-21
- Run Said Rabbi ... p. 45

JEWISH HOLOCAUST POEMS for Mandatory Holocaust Education
- Carmel Forest Fires: Wherever Israelis Go, Gardens Grow ... p. 17
- Jews Live and Die According to God's Divine Plan ... p. 30
- Simon Wiesenthal: Nazi Hunter ... (Design 1 and 2) pp. 32-33, p. 70
- Casting Light: Our Sister Edith Stein of the Star of David ... pp. 34-35
- Sacred Feathers of Divine Freedoms ... p. 36
- Holocaust Denier, Boca Raton, Florida ... p. 37
- My Father's Garden: Eyewitness Account of Child of Holocaust Survivor ... pp. 38-41

Wherever Jews Go, Grass Grows
Wherever Israelis Go, Gardens Grow
—Sharon Esther Lampert

"The worst thing that has ever happened to me was that I was **born**! The best thing that has ever happened to me was that I was born **Jewish**!"

Sharon Esther Lampert
Poet, Prophet, Philosopher, Peacemaker, Paladin of Education, Prodigy

Interesting Note
The IDEA of Sharon Esther Lampert was Born in ISRAEL.
My father survived the Holocaust and went to Israel (10 years).
My mother traveled to Israel on vacation. They met in ISRAEL.
In sum: Both parents had to travel to ISRAEL for me to be born!

BIBLE POEMS
- **WORLD POETRY RECORD** Through the Eyes of Eve (rhyme) ... pp. 22-24
- CAIN'S MARK: Inseparable Together—Alone Forever ... p. 26
- EXODUS — COVID19:The World We Left Behind 2020 ... p. 27
- NOAH'S ARK: Red or White? and the Blues (2017) ... pp. 28-29

JEWISH WOMEN POEMS
- Yael Matzpun: PUSSYWHIPPED (rhyme) ... p. 12
- Bess Myerson: Miss Jewish America ... p. 15
- **WORLD POETRY RECORD** Through the Eyes of Eve (rhyme) ... pp. 22-24
- Casting Light: Our Sister Edith Stein of the Star of David ... pp. 34-35

JEWISH MEMORIAL POEMS
- Mayor Edward Koch: How'm I Doing? (rhyme) ... p. 14
- Rabbi Shlomo Carlbach ... p. 42
- Leiby Kletzky: Abduction, Seduction, Destruction, Reduction, Construction, Deduction... p. 43
- Bring Back Our Boys ... p. 44

JEWISH LOVE POEMS: Poetry Book, "SWEET NOTHINGS"

- TRUE LOVE ... p. 4
- Rabbi Ari: Intimate Blessings (rhyme) ... p. 48
- FIRST LOVE ... p. 49
- THAT KISS (rhyme) ... p. 50
- MY MAN: Making Love All Day and All Night ... p. 51
- Sivan: Melody of F/light (rhyme) ... p. 52
- Marc: Speed of Light (rhyme) ... p. 53
- Rodolfo: The Music, The Muse and The Mystic ... p. 54
- Ziv: Ha-Schechina (rhyme) ... p. 55
- Yossi: The Tow Truck ... p. 56
- Gabriel: Lover Man ... p. 57
- El Shaddai and the Barnes & Noble Poetry Sex Scandal ... pp. 58-59

SEE THE WORLD THOUGH THE EYES OF A CREATIVE GENIUS
- About Sharon Esther Lampert ... pp. 60-62
- One of the World's Greatest Poets ... p. 63
- Sexiest Creative Genius in Human History ... p. 47 and pp. 66-67
- **FAN MAIL** ... pp. 65-73
- National and International Poetry Publications ... pp. 74-75
- WORLD FAMOUS QUOTES ... pp. 76-77
- KADIMAH PRESS: Gifts of Genius ... pp. 78-79
- Count Your Blessings. Practice Gratitude ... p. 80

SEE THE WORLD THROUGH THE

SHARON ESTHER LAMPERT

The
Greatest
Poems
Ever
Written
on
Extraordinary
World
Events

EYES OF A CREATIVE GENIUS

WARNING

KEEP A SAFE DISTANCE OF 6 FEET

HIGH LEVELS OF INTENSITY
INTELLECTUAL COMBUSTION

SHARON ESTHER LAMPERT

PRODIGY

POET, PHILOSOPHER, PROPHET, PEACEMAKER,
PALADIN OF EDUCATION, PHOTON SUPERHERO
PIONEER, PERFORMER, PUBLISHER, PLAYER
PRESIDENT, PHOENIX, PRINCESS of ISRAEL

"The Sole Intention of My Poetry is to Add LIGHT to Your Soul"

"Food is for the Body
Education is for the Mind
Poetry is for the Soul"

"I AM an OPEN Book, to KNOW ME is to READ ME"

"Every Thought in Your Head Was Put There by a Writer"

"When I'm not Writing I'm Reading. When I'm not Writing or Reading, I'm Singing."

"Please Don't Let Me Die with a Typo!"

POE**T**REE

Ink needs a Pen
Pen needs Paper
Paper needs a Poem
Poem needs a Poet
Poet needs a Muse
Muse needs a Poet
Poet needs Divine Inspiration
Divine Inspiration needs Divine Intervention
Divine Intervention needs Divine Grace
Divine Grace needs Immortality
Immortality needs Eternity
Eternity needs Readers of Poetry

By Sharon Esther Lampert

@All Rights Reserved. Sharon Esther Lampert.

YOU HAD TO OUTDO MOSES!
Moses Has 10 Commandments;
You Have 22 Commandments!
—Joel Rapplefeld

SHARON ESTHER LAMPERT
8TH PROPHETESS OF ISRAEL

The 8 Prophetesses of Israel

Sarah
Ageless Beauty, Seer, Holy Spirit
- Genesis 17:15-17:27
- Genesis 18:1-18:15
- Genesis 21:1-21:22
- Genesis 23:1-23:20

Miriam
Saved the life of Moses
- Exodus 2:1-2:10
- Exodus 15:20-15:27
- Numbers 12:1-12:16
- Numbers 20:1-20:6

Deborah
Warrior and 4th Judge
- Judges 4:4-4:14
- Judges 5:1-5:31

Hannah
Personal Prayer
- 1 Samuel 1:1-1:28

Abigail
Prophecy of King David
- 1 Samuel 25:2-25:44
- 1 Samuel 27:1-27:3
- 1 Samuel 30:4
- 2 Samuel 2:2
- 2 Samuel 3:2

Huldah
Learning, Enlightenment, and Peace
- 2 Kings 22:1-20

Esther
Rescued Jews from Genocide
- Esther 2:7-2:23
- Esther 4:1-4:16
- Esther 5:1-5:8
- Esther 7:1-7:10
- Esther 8:3-8:8
- Esther 9:12-9:14
- Esther 9:26-9:32

Sharon Esther Lampert
- 22 Commandments
- World Peace Equation
- 40 Absolute Truths
- World Poetry Record
- 40 Universal Gold Standards of Education
- 22 Steps to Find a Soulmate
- 10 Thinking Tools of Creative Genius

All You Will Ever Need to Know About God
The 22 Commandments
A Universal Moral Compass For All People, For All Religions, and For All Time

1. **LIFE** Over Death
2. **STRENGTH** Over Weakness
3. **DEED** Over Sin
4. **LOVE** Over Hatred
5. **TRUTH** Over Lie
6. **WISDOM** Over Stupidity
7. **OPTIMISM** Over Pessimism
8. **SHARING** Over Selfishness
9. **PRAISE** Over Criticism
10. **LOYALTY** Over Abandonment
11. **RESPONSIBILITY** Over Blame
12. **GRATITUDE** Over Envy
13. **REWARD** Over Punishment
14. **DEMOCRACY** Over Domination
15. **CREATION** Over Destruction
16. **EDUCATION** Over Ignorance
17. **COOPERATION** Over Competition
18. **FREEDOM** Over Oppression
19. **COMPASSION** Over Indifference
20. **FORGIVENESS** Over Revenge
21. **PEACE** Over War
22. **JOY** Over Suffering

"Moses had 10 commandments. You have 22 commandments. You had to out do Moses."
Joel Rapplefeld

"Inside Every Jewish Person Is a Little Moses Tying to Get Out."
Chabad Rabbi Ben Tzion Krasnianski

Sharon Esther Lampert
KADIMAH
8TH Prophetess of Israel

Learn It. Live It. Share It.

1. Sarah: (Genesis 21:12) Ageless Beauty, Seer, Holy Spirit
2. Miriam: Exodus 15:21 Saved the life of Moses
3. Devorah: Judges 4:4 Warrior and 4th Judge
4. Chanah: I Samuel 2:1-10 Personal Prayer
5. Abigail: I Samuel (25:2-44) Prophecy of King David
6. Huldah: Kings 22:14 Learning, Enlightenment, and Peace
7. Esther: The Book of Esther Saved the Jews from Genocide
8. Kadimah: 22 Commandments Beauty, Seer, Holy Spirit, Learning, Englightenment and World Peace

@All Rights Reserved. Sharon Esther Lampert.com

#1 Poetry Website for Student Projects

True Love

True Love is Unconditional.
True Love is Found in the Deed.
True Love is Found in the We.
True Love Joins the Heart,
Mind, and Body as One.

By Sharon Esther Lampert

BE ART

ART IS SMART
ART IS OF THE HEART
MAKE ART NOT WAR
YOU ARE BORN FOR GREATNESS
YOR ARE A MASTERPIECE

SHARON ESTHER LAMPERT
www.sharonestherlampert.com

#1 Poetry Website for Student Projects

WORLD PEACE EQUATION
VG+VL=VP

Virtue of the Good + Value of Life = Vision of Peace

The Mathematical and Philosophical Proof for World Peace

$$VG + VL = VP$$
$$VP = VG + VL$$
$$VP = V(G+L)$$
$$P = (G+L)$$
$$\text{Peace} = \text{Good} + \text{Life}$$
$$\text{Peace} = \text{Good Life}$$

Gift Shop: WorldPeaceEquation.com

@All Rights Reserved. Sharon Esther Lampert.

My gifts did not come with an instruction manual. There were no teachers to guide me, and no classes to teach how to maximize my creative potential. I am its servant and messenger, and the instrument of its desires and destiny!

Sharon Esther Lampert

Poet
Prophet
Philosopher
Paladin of Education
Peacemaker
Princess Kadimah
Prodigy
PINUP

How to Read a Poem by Sharon Esther Lampert

1. Sharon's Poetry Paintings
Similar to the poet William Blake, her poems are accompanied by elaborate visual graphics that enrich and compliment the text. The poems are wall hangings, and her poems are framed by ardent fans and hang in their living spaces, like paintings. Students, the world over, read her poems in their classrooms, and use her poetry for their school assignments.

2. Sharon is a Master of Condensation
Sharon is a master of the art of condensation. She is able to condense a major world event in world history into a one-page poem. Her immortal literary gems come in a variety of lengths: A single sentence, a single page, and grand sweeping epics.

3. Sharon Is a Literary Photographer
Her poems are telescopic of the main event and microscopic of the infinite details.

4. Sharon Can Pack a Single Verse
Sharon's poems are known for her ability to weave poetry, philosophy, and comedy into a single verse.

5. Documentary Poet: Poems are Cinematic Journey's Through History
Sharon's poems take you on a cinematic journey, and make you feel as if you are reliving the event, as if it happened today.

6. Sharon's Poems Are Completed Literary Works
Many poets leave abandoned poems that went unfinished. Sharon's poems are completed works of art. Every word is essential to the poem. You cannot remove or replace a word. There are no extra words. Every word has its rightful place and fits to perfection.

7. Sharon's Poems Are All Inspired Works of Art
All of her poems are inspired. There are no rough drafts. Like giving birth to a baby, the poem incubates in her extra-body part a "Creative Apparatus" and is birthed in minutes. Like a baby, the poems are delivered whole and complete.

8. Sharon's Signature Endings: The Epiphany (Spiritual Illumination)
Quote: "The Sole Intention of My Poetry Is to Add LIGHT to Your Soul"
The last verse of every poem delivers a message that educates, enlightens, and empowers. Her searing signature endings find their way into your heart, open your mind to a deeper understanding, and stay with you forever.

©2000. All Rights Reserved. Sharon Esther Lampert.
FAN MAIL: FANS@SharonEstherLampert.com

PUBLICATION

בס"ד

Vol. VII No. 3   BERESHITH "IN THE BEGINNING"   *Nisan 5754/March 1994*

MY JEWISH ESSENCE

by Sharon Esther Lampert

Anti-Semitism is a weed.

The weed is found in Jewish gardens.

Jewish gardens have Jewish plants.

Jewish plants are identified by Jewish roots.

Jewish roots are grounded in Jewish traditions.

Jewish traditions nourish Jewish plants with Jewish nutrients.

Jewish nutrients are Jewish spiritual messages that pass from generation to generation in the form of Torah, rabbinic interpretation, legal codes, poetry, precept, parable, prayer and song.

Jewish spiritual messages transmit a steady stream of life sustaining and enhancing instructions that allow Jewish plants to survive, thrive, and flourish in the midst of wars, invasions, exiles and persecutions.

Inherent in the instructions is G-ds gift to the Jewish people.

This gift protects Jewish life through time.

This is the Jewish gift to the world as witnessed by the history of the world.

This gift is indestructible as its power is its essence.

The essence of the gift has the power to transform the world.

It is the gift of choosing life.

Sharon Esther Lampert is a member of the Beginners Service at Congregation Kehilath Jeshurun in New York.

Illustrations by Florie Freshman

בראשית   Bereshith: "In the Beginning" is edited under the direction of *Beryl Levenson* of the **National Jewish Outreach Program**, Inc. Special Beginners Services are conducted at synagogues throughout the United States to introduce those with limited backgrounds to the beauty of the traditional Hebrew service. For more information regarding the Beginners Service closest to your home, to establish a local Beginners Service, or to learn more about programs of the NJOP, please write or call: 485 Fifth Avenue, Suite 212, New York, NY 10017, (212) 986-7450.

Readers: This is your newsletter, and we'd like to hear from you. Article contributions are always welcome.

200 AMSTERDAM AVENUE
NEW YORK, N.Y. 10023

```
PRE-SORTED
FIRST CLASS MAIL
U.S.POSTAGE
PAID
NEW YORK, N.Y.
PERMIT NO. 4666
```

My Jewish Essence

Anti-Semitism is a Weed.
The Weed Usurps Jewish Gardens.
Jewish Gardens Embody Jewish Plants.
Jewish Plants are Distinguished by Jewish Roots.
Jewish Roots are Grounded in Jewish Traditions.

Jewish Traditions Fortify Jewish Plants Providing Jewish Spiritual Nourishment.
Jewish Spiritual Nourishment Imparts Jewish Ethical Instructions Implanted By;
Talmud of Mishnah and Gemara; Midrash, Aggadah, Halakhah
Dvar Torah, Parable, Precept, Poem, Prayer and Song.

These Jewish Ethical Instructions are God's Gift for the Jewish people.
Jewish Ethical Instructions Impart Virtuous Mitzvot,
Between God and Humanity,
Between Humanity and Humanity,
And Between an Individual Soul and Itself.

These Mitzvot Pass Manifest from Generation to Generation,
From Righteous and Loving Grandparents,
To Devout and Devoted Parents,
To Respectful and Joyful Children.

These Jewish Ethical Instructions are the Jewish Gift for the World
As Witnessed by the History of the World.
Jewish Ethical Instructions Transmit a Steady Stream
Of Life Sustaining and Enhancing Jewish Spiritual Messages,
Protecting, Shielding, and Sheltering The Jewish People,
Allowing the Jewish People to Survive, Thrive, and Flourish
In the Midst of Merciless, Enforced, Religious Conversions,
Enforced Relentless Explusions, Deportations and Exiles,
Willfully Descending Silently into Unspeakable Depravity,
By Enforced, Forced, and Reinforced Remorseless Geoncide.

God's Gift Protects Jewish Life through Time.
God's Gift has the Power to Transform the World.
God's Gift is Indestructible; its Power is its Essence.

The Essence of God's Gift is the Perennial Spiritual Sustenance
Of the Fortifying Jewish Ethical Instruction to Sanctify Life in this World.

#1 Poetry Website for Student Projects

WORLD FAMOUS POEM
Astronaut Ilan Ramon: Space Legacy of a Legend
JUST HEAVEN EXISTS

THE SOLE INTENTION OF MY POETRY IS TO ADD LIGHT TO YOUR SOUL.

"My heartfelt condolences to all of the bereaved families of the astronauts:
Rick Husband, William McCool, Michael Anderson, David Brown, Ilan Ramon, Kalpana Chawla, and Laurel Clark."
S. E. Lampert

Space Legacy of a Legend

Astronaut Ilan Ramon
(1954-2003)

On January 16, 2003, we were all certain that Astronaut Ilan Ramon would **JUST** pull away the final curtain.

In good company, floating forever among the billions of bright stars,
The colonel is **JUST** one more pioneer, among many Israeli pioneers,
who have crossed, are crossing, and will cross unimaginable frontiers.

He rode the Columbia rocket STS-107 up into the dark and dreamy
Heavens, to catch **JUST** one more twinkling star and cast it down,
To humankind, to show the scientific possibility,
That a **JUST** heaven exists, for all of us to see.

He JUST Did What He Loved and We JUST Loved What He Did:
1. First: Israeli in space, for 16 days glory was his.
2. First: One-man operation to lift the spirits of the entire nation of Israel.
3. First: Citizen to cast his ballot in an Israeli election and vote in space.
4. First: Israeli national flag in space.
5. First: Israeli "Declaration of Independence" in space.
6. First: T-shirt from the Israeli Road Safety Campaign in space.
7. First: Recitation of the "Shema" prayer
8. First: To celebrate Shabbat (occurs every 10 1/2 hrs.) in space.
9. First: Kiddush cup and mezuzah in space.
10. First: Kosher meal in space.
11. First: Dr. Joachim Joseph's Bar-Mitzvah Torah (Bergen Belsen) in space.
12. First: Holocaust artwork, "Moon Landscape" by Peter Ginz (Thresienstadt), in space.
13. First: Picture from Yad Vashem in space.
14. First: Study of how near-zero gravity affects the growth of crystals (Ort Technical H.S.).
15. First: Mediteranean Israeli Dust Experiment(MEIDEX) in space (Tel Aviv University).
16. First: Ilan Ramon's personal journal was recovered at the site of the crash.

Peter Ginz

Age 14, Theresienstadt ghetto, Murdered in Auschwitz in 1944.

"Moon Landscape"

He Had It All and JUST Risked It All, In A Fall:
Miracle baby, child of a Holocaust survivor, living in his own homeland,
A 2000-year miracle, a dream-come-true, at long last, a happy past.
Courageous war hero, he bombed an Iraqi demon, the Osiraq reactor;
Victories abound, Yom Kippur and Lebanon Wars: he is a prime factor.
Loving wife Rona and four beloved children: Assaf, David, Tal, and Noa,
No room for mamma's boys, his heart was full and filled with joys.

His Labor of Love Was Great; His JUST Reward, A Matter of Fate:
Everlasting, within the infinite cosmos, he lives eternally missed: **We send up a kiss.**
He stared down the demons of death many times, and finally, living his dream,
He died doing what he loved, a divine kiss on a life-long dream gone amiss,
Last orbit, over Israel, a dust plume is in bloom, or is it a premonition of a tomb?
Leaving no trace of doom or gloom, 255 orbits in a row, his flickering starlight in tow,
Dualities of gladness and sadness; a change in climate -- a new dust storm is born.
A 9:16 landing: **JUST** 16 minutes away from the millions of loving arms of
Family and fans: our hearts broken, in an abyss, the bittersweet memory of
The space legacy and the legend of Astronaut Ilan Ramon persist,
Even in a universe where destiny resists, fate twists, and cruelty insists;
We are still certain, that behind the final curtain,
A **JUST** Heaven Exists.

Space Stamp

JEWISH ASTRONAUTS IN SPACE
1. Dr. Judith A. Resnick: Discovery, Challenger (First Jewish Astronaut)
2. Dr. Scott J. Horowitz: Columbia, Discovery, and Atlantis
3. Dr. Ellen S. Baker: Atlantis, Columbia
4. Dr. Jay Apt: Atlantis, Endeavor
5. Dr. Jeffrey A. Hoffman: Discovery, Columbia, Atlantis, and Endeavor
6. Dr. David A. Wolf: Endeavor (Dreidel Spinning in Mid-Air from Zero Gravity)
7. Colonel Ilan Ramon: Columbia (1st Israeli in space)

THEME OF POEM: NASA **JUST** needs to find us a new planet to live on that has love, mercy, justice, equality, and compassion. This poem remembers and records all the thrills and chills of space travel.

KABBALISTIC THOUGHT
Q: Is there a deeper meaning encoded in the coincidences of the number 16?
- January 16th, 2003
- 16 days in space
- 9:16 landing
- 16 mins. left (disaster)
- 16x16 = 256 (orbits)
- 16 vital contributions

NASA DISASTERS
1. Apollo, January 27, 1967 (3 Astronauts)
2. Challenger, January 28, 1986 (7 Astronauts)
3. Columbia, February 1, 2003 (7 Astronauts)

Sharon Esther Lampert
Sexiest Creative Genius in Human History
8th Prophetess of Israel: 22 Commandments

www.PoetryJewels.com
Diamonds, Emeralds, Sapphires, Rubies, and Pearls

Todah Rabah to My Darling Muse Yoram

#1 Poetry Website for Student Projects

Athens, Greece, August 25, 2004

THE GREATEST POEM EVER WRITTEN ON
Gal Friedman: Gold MeGal

Israel's First Olympic Gold Medal

In Loving Memory of the 11 Israeli Athletes Murdered at the 1972 Olympic Games in Germany:
David Berger, Zeev Friedman, Yossef Gutfreund, Elizer Halfin, Yossef Romano, Amitzur Shapira, Kehat Shorr, Mark Slavin, Andre Spitzer, Jacov Springer, Moshe Weinberg.

Gal Friedman braves the vast expanse of the Aegean sea on a sail,
For an Olympic dream of glory, tactically flawless, without fail.
At his back, only a chattering wind, a squinting sun, and a buoyant wave,
He is hungry for an Olympic gold medal, that is all the athletic rave.
A windsurfing phenomenon in Atlanta, a bronze medal is in the bag.
He sings the beautiful "Hatikva" (The Hope), and hoists up the Israeli flag.
For the first time in 52 years, there is a momentary freedom from fears.
"Mazel Tov!, Mazel Tov! " an olive-branch wreath sits on his head.
"Hellas!, Hellas!" our next-door Greek neighbor cheeringly said.
Still in his prime, at 29, he said, "I knew the gold medal was mine."
Tears of joy stream down his handsome and sunburnt face.
Gold-Medal Gal is the great champion of the windsurfing race.

Topping Nikolaos Kaklamanakis of Greece,
Nick Dempsey of Britain, and Ricardo Santos of Brazil,
Gold Medal Gal of Israel, wraps himself in our Israeli flag,
And becomes the first-ever Israeli athlete, in 12 Olympics to
Give our beloved nation of beleaguered Jewish heroes a thrill.
His family and fans yelled, "C'mon Gal," "Yalla, Yalla, Yalla."
On his surfboard, lands a white dove, a sign of peace from way up above.
All of Israel had stopped to watch the race,
Gold-Medal Gal delivers the gold, a divine gift of grace.

Gal means "wave" in Hebrew, and his fate and destiny are intertwined.
Waves of emotion overflow and flood the media airwaves with joy and
Pride, and great relief, from the Olympic tragedy of another time:
At the 1972 games in Munich, 11 innocent Israeli athletes and coaches were kidnapped and
Murdered by Black September Palestinian terrorists who play an evil game to achieve their fame.
Gal Friedman was not yet born, however, our country's heart was deeply torn.
Ready for Action: lining the waterfront, soldiers tote machine guns and are ready to run.

In a change of wind, Olympic dreams live in split seconds of glory that last a lifetime,
Or die in split seconds of defeat, drowning the dream in a silent scream.
Every Olympian waits to see the results: will I be happy or will I be sad?
Did I break a world record or will I be mad? Will I have to explain my defeat
On missing a beat to the hysterical Yenta Central media?
Or will my mother see my fabulous finish on the front cover…
Of the Jerusalem Post and The New York Times?
Will Prime Minister Sharon call to congratulate me on my gain,
Or will my Coach Gur Steinberg share my four lost years of injury and pain?
Extreme focus. The pressure is peaking. He is the embodiment of a national hero.
Ready for Action: Gal Friedman delivers the gold, and Israel has a joy to behold.

Mistral, the official name for the event, is a 4.24-meter, or 13-foot-11-inch, long fiberglass windsurfing board weighing 15.4 kilograms, or 34 pounds, and with a 7.4-square-meter, or 80-square-foot, sail. It was introduced at the 1996 Olympics.

ISRAEL'S OLYMPIC MEDALS
1. Yael Arad's Silver Medal in Judo in 1992.
2. Oren Smadja's Bronze Medal in Judo in 1992.
3. Gal Friedman's Bronze Medal in Windsurfing in 1996.
4. Michael Kalganov's Bronze Medal in Kayaking in 2000.
5. Arik Zeevi's Bronze Medal in Judo in 2004.
6. Gal Friedman's Gold Medal in Windsurfing in 2004.

Sharon Esther Lampert
Sexiest Creative Genius in Human History
8th Prophetess of Israel: 22 Commandments
Todah Rabah to Karl, My Darling Muse

www.PoetryJewels.com
Diamonds, Emeralds, Sapphires, Rubies, and Pearls

#1 Poetry Website for Student Projects

SEE THE WORLD THROUGH THE EYES OF A CREATIVE GENIUS

www.WorldFamousPoems.com

The Greatest Poems Ever Written on Extraordinary World Events

PUSSYWHIPPED

Sdel Avaraham, Israel November 28, 2012

Heroine Israeli Mother Yael Matzpun
Scared, Scarred, and Split Decisions

He has heavy footprints and turns on the light.
It is 3 A.M., and a Muslim terrorist in a kefiyyeh is
Thirsty for the Jewish blood of innocents, and is in for a fight.

Get up ! he orders and lie down on the floor! She has other
plans and traps him behind a barricaded bathroom door.

He pushes her on the bed and slashes her pretty face.
The IDF will shoot him dead, closing the murderous case.

Memories of Itamar and the massacre of the Fogel Family haunted.
Yael fiercely fights him off and protects her four kids undaunted.

Dancing to death, he throws things at her, a mirror and a scale.
She picks up a heavy metal horse ball, and he turns yellow and pale.

He climbs out the bathroom window in a thin skin.
The bully on the outside is always a coward within.

Years ago, in fact, I took a class in Israeli Krav Maga hand to hand combat,
But decided I prefer a loaded gun as not to ruin my manicure on a dirty rat.

By Sharon Esther Lampert

"Food Is For the Body,
Education Is for the Mind,
and Poetry Is for the Soul."

Pussy-whipped: Today Palestinians are unable to celebrate their fallen martry's disgrace and horror.
Tomorrow Yael's children and grandchildren will celebrate **Matzpun Street** named in her honor.

The Sole Intention of My Poetry Is to Add LIGHT to Your Soul

#1 Poetry Website for Student Projects
www.WorldFamousPoems.com
The Greatest Poems Ever Written on Extraordinary World Events

Sharon Esther Lampert
Princess Kadimah
8TH Prophetess of Israel
The 22 Commandments
Books:
Immortality Is Mine
Poetry Jewels
Sweet Nothings
V.E.S.S.E.L.

October 3rd, 2009

*"Food Is for the Body
Education Is for the Mind
And Poetry Is for the Soul"
Sharon Esther Lampert*

Shalom Sergeant Shalit

Like a caged bird, Gilad yearns to be free
He sits and reads middle east politics
He walks and talks middle east politics
He eats and sleeps middle east politics

. . . Tic-Tock, Tic-Tock, Tic-Tock . . .

Same shit, different day: It is September 14, 2009
Three years ago, in a cross-border raid, he paid

. . . Tic-Tock, Tic-Tock, Tic-Tock . . .

Shalom Shalit, Shalit Shalom

Peace for Piece: One victorious Israel and 23 hostile Arab nations
Tit for Tat: One Sabra Gilad for 1000 dangerous Palestinian prisoners
Same shit, different day: Israel's nuclear bomb keeps the peace

. . . Tic-Tock, Tic-Tock, Tic-Tock . . .

60 Years in a beautiful Jewish homeland
An imperfect peace in an imperfect world

. . . Tic-Tock, Tic-Tock, Tic-Tock . . .

Shalom Shalit, Shalit Shalom

The Sole Intention of My Poetry Is to Add LIGHT to Your Soul

#1 Poetry Website for Student Projects

www.WorldFamousPoems.com
The Greatest Poems Ever Written on Extraordinary World Events

E-Mail: gosmart@earthlink.net, Phone: (212)772-0326

"How'm I Doing?"

Your tombstone is driving New Yorkers crazy.
They can't remember your middle name.
You're alive and well, but who can tell?

Your tombstone stands tall and proud of
Your Hebrew race, and it bears a quote
From a beheaded Jewish face: David Pearl.
You're alive and well, but who can tell?

Prickly New Yorkers will most likely stop, stare, and say,
"I never liked Koch, but I am going to miss him."
All kidding aside, in Newark, they may honor you one day
With an E.I.K. Airport, that sort of rhymes, with J.F.K.
You're alive and well, but who can tell?

The towering, baldheaded Jew boy from the Bronx made good
Because the war veteran, congressman, and mayor understood
That loose ends can sink a ship and destroy an economy.
So please inscribe your candid remark, **"How'm I Doing?"**
On the backside of your tombstone, while you're alive
and well, but who can tell?

That courageous, in your face, remark, **"How'm I Doing?"**
Will get crabby and cranky New Yorkers talking out loud
About how you made us all so very proud.
You presented me with an award at City Hall, I recall.
The first Jewish boy who was taller than me, I see.
You're alive and well, but who can tell?

Sharon Esther Lampert
Poet, Philosopher, Paladin of Education,
Peacemaker, Pioneer, PIN-Up, and Prophet
The Sexiest Creative Genius in Human His

www.PoetryJewels.com
Diamonds, Emeralds, Sapphires, Rubies, and Pearls

Books:
Immortality Is Mine
Sweet Nothings: 40 Love Poems
Creative Insanity
V.E.S.S.E.L.
Green Thumb Poetry Pointers
Intelligent Beach Bum's Poetry Journal

Posthumously:
An iconoclast, "Mayor for Life" Koch buried himself in a non-denominational
Church cemetery, shunning family, faith, and friends, what a pity,
To be close to his one and only true love: New York City.

New York City breeds eccentric loners who crave their aloneness --
We prefer to wander the hallowed halls of the American Museum of Natural History
To try to understand nature's intricate, unfathomable, and infinite mystery.

And so, after all was said, one final loose end, remained undone:
A nameless airport in Newark that badly needs an honorable name, is his last wish;
EDWARD IRVING KOCH AIRPORT, aka, E.I.K. AIRPORT

#1 Poetry Website for Student Projects

www.WorldFamousPoems.com
The Greatest Poems Ever Written on Extraordinary World Events

"Food is for the Body, Education is for the Mind, And Poetry is for the Soul" SEL

You Can't Be Beautiful and Hate

By Sharon Esther Lampert, Jan 11, 2015

Jewish Miss America

Sept. 8, 1945 --
Bess Myerson, the first and
Only **Jewish Miss America**:
Beauty, brains, and musical
Talent galore was a beacon of
LIGHT in 1945, as **EVIL** minds
And murderous **NAZI** monsters gassed
Six million innocent Jewish souls.

Bess was much more than big tits,
Long legs, tight ass, and a gorgeous
Face, she was educated, at Hunter.
As beauty is deaf, dumb, and blind; Bess
Rose above ethnic and racial bigotry.
Smart women are bitches, not babes.

Bess went to work in a man's world;
And played dirty politics in the filthy
Political sand box of injustice. Bess
Faltered: She lost a senate election,
She lost at love, of two husbands,
And she lost her health to ovarian cancer.
Scandal dimmed her starlight: **THE BESS MESS**.
Bess was acquitted of all charges and **WON**.
Bess got caught shoplifting nail polish and **LOST**.

Falling from grace; her beauty no
Longer able to pay the bills; Her
Education, a complete waste, when
Face to face with street smarts;
Her friends no longer basking in her
SPOTLIGHT; her brains no longer able
To rise above adversity, the roller
Coaster ride of highs and lows; "Weeeeeeeeeeeeeeeeee"
Broke her: mind, body, and soul. Reality is a **BITCH**.

Another educated damsel in distress: **Hilliary Clinton**
Rose above financial scandals, infidelity,
And political minefields badly bruised
With emotional safety nets of Mother
And Daughter, **LOYAL** through thick-N-thin.
Face to face with sexism, steely eyed, Hillary
Rises daily above the **HATE** to serve America.
President Abraham Lincoln said, **"Hater's Gonna Hate."**

Bess failed to rise above her mistakes and
Misfortunes, and her blessings of beauty,
Brains, and talent leave **JEWS** bewildered: **WHY?**
Bess moved out of the spotlight into obsurity.
An emotional safety net, her **LOYAL (unconditional love)**
Daughter was the only **LIGHT** in her life, till age 90.
Men want loyal sons; Women want loyal daughters.

2016: We have waited eight years for Hilliary Clinton
To rise again and take the reigns and run for
President of America. She can't fix a broken world because
"It Takes a Village," but she is the **ONE** to break the oval
Office glass ceiling. Hillary has logged millions of global miles;
She is covered in wrinkles and is now called Grandma.
Game on. Hate on. Hillary's got nothing left to lose.

*"The Sole Intention of MY Poetry, Is to Add **LIGHT** to Your Soul"* By Sharon Esther Lampert

www.WorldFamousPoems.com
#1 Poetry Website for Student Projects
The Greatest Poems Ever Written on Extraordinary World Events

The Militant Palestinian Toddler Terrorist

At my mother's breast
I learned how to thirst for the blood of Jews

Other toddlers learn how to live and love
I will learn how to hate Jews and die as a martyr

Other toddlers have parents that love them
My parents love to hate Jews

Other toddlers wear blue and pink
I wear a belt packed with explosives to kill Jews

Other toddlers love to cuddle adorable stuffed animals
I love to clench rocks to throw at Israeli soldiers

Other toddlers have a favorite blanket
I love to stomp on and burn American and Israeli flags

Other toddlers love to play games and laugh out loud
I have a toy chest filled with loud katyusha rockets that make Jews cry

Today I plan to kill Jewish mothers and fathers and tonight
We will all be together in heaven

In heaven I will know the love of a Jewish mother and father
And I will rest in peace

1989 (1 attack)
1990s
1993 (2 bombings)
1994 (5 bombings)
1995 (4 bombings)
1996 (4 bombings)
1997 (3 bombings)
1998 (2 bombings)
1999 (2 bombings)
2000s
2000 (5 bombings)
2001 (40 bombings)
2002 (47 bombings)
2003 (23 bombings)
2004 (17 bombings)
2005 (9 bombings)
2006 (3 bombings)
2007 (1 bombing)
2008 (2 bombings)
2015 (1 bombing)

@All Rights Reserved. Sharon Esther Lampert.

#1 Poetry Website for Student Projects

SEE THE WORLD THROUGH THE EYES OF A CREATIVE GENIUS

#1 Poetry Website for Teacher Lesson Plans and Student Projects
www.WorldFamousPoems.com
The Greatest Poems Ever Written on Extraordinary World Events

KADIMAH
8TH
PROPHETESS
ISRAEL

Wherever Israelis Go, Gardens Grow
Hanukkah & Israel's Mount Carmel Fire, December 2-6, 2010

By Prodigy Sharon Esther Lampert

For 4 of the 8 days of Hanukah,
The God of Moses did not show her face
And blow out the conflagration.

Prophet Elijah, who resides in
A cave on its slopes, did not
Offer his wise counsel.

A mighty Israeli heroine, Brigadier
General Ahuva Tomer, waged
Her last battle, and was consumed.

Just a teen sapling, Elad Riven,
Waged his first heroic battle and
Was consumed. If only his mother's
Tears could extinguish the fire in his heart.

Fires race to the treetops and create walls.
The flames are fierce, furious, and fearless.
They show no mercy for man, beast, or flower.

Dry combustible wood and strong
Winds feverishly incinerate the
Living into black soot and ash.

Billows of smoke blanket the sky, like
Crematoria of six German gas chambers:
**Kiryat Bialik, Tirat Hacarmel, Denya
Beit Oren, Usfiya, and Ein Hod.**

The oak tree's roots are buried
Deep beneath the ground,
And they will rise again.

The Aleppo pine cones eject
Their winged seeds and settle in
The soil elsewhere, to rise again.

A bus is burned beyond recognition AS
IF blown to bits by Palestinian suicide
Bombers. Dental remains of 42 *Security Forces*
Will confirm their existence and fill their coffins.
30 children have lost the love of a parent.
Is Efrat Cohen's engagement ring redeemable?

During the Holocaust, the Jews cried out,
And everyone heard, but no one listened,
And six million Jews perished. It is Hanukah,
The season of a miracle, yet unfathomable.

Five million Jewish trees have perished.
**Wherever Jews Go, Grass Grows;
Wherever Israelis Go, Gardens Grow.**
There are no mighty Jewish warriors who
Will come to her rescue with the help of the
Outstretched hand of God, to perform a miracle.
It is a national trauma. Israeli power is powerless.

So **ISRAEL** cries out to the nations of the world,
And for the outstretched hand of the God of
Gentiles, and they saturate her air space with
Their birds of steel: In 24 hours, 10 airplanes are
In the air dousing the flames. In 48 hours, 33
airplanes are in the air, dousing the flames, and
16 more are en route ready to douse the flames.

12 Gentile nations, like brothers, come out
Of the heavens, and vanquish her enemy.
Israel has real friends, who are not fellow Jews,
Living among the Gentiles, but Gentiles who
Heard her cry out in pain, in her own homeland,
And came to her aid after her first tear was shed.
This is the **MIRACLE** that occurred on Hanukah.
 This Hanukah we usher in a new **AGE OF PEACE**.

1. Greece 2. Turkey 3. Netherlands 4. Belgium 5. Germany 6. Finland 7. Norway 8. Russia 9. Switerland 10. Cyprus 11. United Kingdom 12. USA EVERGREEN 747 SUPERTANKER

#1 Poetry Website for Student Projects

AUGUST 15th, 2005
GAZA STRIP WITHDRAWAL
55,000 ISRAELI SOLDIERS
9,000 Settlers and 21 Settlements

21 Jewish Settlements	Year Established	2004 Population
Nasanit	1984	1016
Elei Sinai	1983	407
Dugit	1990	79
Netzarim	1972	496
Kfar Darom	1970	491
Netzer Hazani	1973	461
Katif	1985	404
Ganei Tal	1979	400
Tel Katifa	1992	60
Shirat Hayam	2000	40
Kfar Yam	1983	10
Neve Dekalim	1983	2671
Gadid	1982	351
Gan Or	1983	351
Peat' Sadeh	1989	104
Slav	2001	50
Rafiah Yam	1984	143
Morag	1982	221
Atzmona	1982	646
Kerem Atzmona	2001	24
Bedolah	1986	219

1000.000 PALESTINIANS AND 8 PALESTINAIN REFUGEE CAMPS:
JABALIA
SHATI
NUSEIRAT
BUREIG
DEIR AL-BALAH
AL-MAGHAZI
KHAN YAUNIS
RAFAH

7 BORDER CROSSINGS:
EREZ
NAHIL
OZ
KARNI
KISSUFIM
SUFA
KEREM

#1 Poetry Website for Student Projects

THE SOLE INTENTION OF MY POETRY IS TO ADD LIGHT TO YOUR SOUL

THE GREATEST POEM EVER WRITTEN ON THE GAZA STRIP WITHDRAWAL, AUGUST 15th, 2005

© N.Y.T.

SALAHADIN ROAD

SALAHADIN is the main highway in the Gaza Strip. The word means "The Righteousness of the Faith." Saladin was a 12th century Kurdish Muslim military general.

Sharon Esther Lampert
Sexiest Creative Genius in Human History
8th Prophetess of Israel: 22 Commandments

www.PoetryJewels.com
Diamonds, Emeralds, Sapphires, Rubies, and Pearls

Todah Rabah to Karl, My Darling Muse
Written on August 18th, 2005
© All Rights Reserved

The Arab National Dream of the "**23 Nation United-Arab Empire**" Dissolved into Tears.
The Arab National Dream of Throwing the Jews into the Sea Dissolved into Fears.

Israel's National Dream of the "**One Greater Israel-God's Biblical Promise**" Dissolved into Tears.
Israel's National Dream of Exiling the Palestinians into "**JORDAN IS PALESTINE**" Dissolved into Fears.

Israel Plants the Settlers as an Ideological Seed.
Palestinians Plant the Suicide Bombers as the Evil Deed.
Israel Plants Closures, Seizures, and Blockades to Halt the Mangled Bleed.
Palestinians Plant Their Children in Bloodthirsty Baths to Fulfill Their Political Need.
Paying for the Sins of Your Parents, Child Abuse, is a Universal Creed.
Israel Plants Democracy, Civil Rights, and Personal Liberty into the Middle East, the Great Deed.
Israel Plants Her Fertile Seed into the Barren Gaza Desert, and Green Gardens Grow, That Feed.
Israel Plants Her Capital in Jerusalem, "The City of David-1000 B.C." and All Religions Pray for Peace to Succeed.
Palestinians Plant a National Flag into the Hands of Thugs, the Weeds, Who Negotiate with Terror, the Error.

Across the Tumultuous Desert of Stormy and Raging Sands of Infinite Land:
21 Jewish Settlements and 8 Palestinian-Refugee Camps and 1,000.000 Palestinians are Scattered,
Their Loved Ones Who Mattered are Splattered,
Two Peoples have had Their Hearts Shattered.

Jewish Settlers Appear as Pioneers,
Jewish Settlers Disappear as Mutineers.
Evacuating 9,000 Jews from Their Own Homeland,
55,000 Israeli Soldiers Face New Frontiers.

   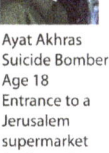

Ayat Akhras
Suicide Bomber
Age 18
Entrance to a
Jerusalem
supermarket
April 2, 2002

Palestinian Children Dressed as Terrorists and Suicide Bombers
Child Abuse: The Next Generation of Cripples, Parasites, and Predators

Can Both Peoples Pick up the Remaining Pieces of Their Tattered Hearts that are Broken and Bleeding for 57 Years?

Can Both Peoples Rebuild the Two-Aching Chambers Across the Biblical Frontiers,
From a 5000-Year Old, Archeological-Excavation Site of Unlimited Supplies of Paleolithic Spears,
Laying Down Their Ancient Weapons, and Hardened Hearts Filled with Tears and Fears…
To Start Selling Neolithic-Tourist Souvenirs.

Can Both Peoples Resew Their Steadfast Hearts Seamlessly, Side by Side, Along the Jagged Edges?
For Two Peoples Who Have to Share One Heart Alleges, and Pledges:
A True Love of Their Respective Homeland is Grand.

Two Nations are Forlorn.
One Nation is Reborn.

#1 Poetry Website for Student Projects

EPIC POEM
In 5 Minutes
Learn 5000 Years of Jewish History

By Sharon Esther Lampert -In Celebration of 50TH Birthday

Many Jews Reclaimed God

By Divine Words and Divine Works, Abraham and Sarah, Isaac and Rebecca, Jacob, Leah, and Rachel conceived a holy people. Familiar family faith. In an ark, Noah was not consumed; a rainbow ascended. Adam blamed Eve, and the Garden of Eden was left behind. Joseph cast into a pit and prison, was recast as a prince of Egypt. The silver goblet ascended. Benjamin was not left behind. Familiar family forgiveness. Divine convenants of spiritual and physical dimensions were contracted with Abraham, Noah, Jacob, and Moses. Seven prophetesses ascended: Sarah, Miriam, Deborah, Hannah, Abigail, Huldah and Esther; the first beauty queen contestant. All Hebrews became physically and spiritually enslaved in Egypt; mortar descended and bricks ascended. GOD spoke to Moses and Moses once-and-once-again received The Ten Commandments. The burning bush was not consumed. Twelve tribes ascended. All of the Children of Israel received The **Ten Commandments** in the barren desert. Many Jews became spiritually liberated.
MANY JEWS HAD FOUND GOD

All Jews wanted physical deliverance from the barren desert. Many Jews found the homeland and became Israelites, a miracle. Moses was left behind. All Jews were divided into two kingdoms: Northern Kingdom of Israel in Samaria and Southern Davidic Kingdom of Judah in Judea. Some Jews remained Jews after the Assyrian exile, Babylonian exile, and destruction of the First Temple. Some Jews remained Jews after the Roman exile and destruction of the Second Temple. King Saul, King David, and King Solomon ascended. Ascending and descending, messiahs, miracles, and martyrs were left behind. All Canaanite, Philistine, Ammonite, Moabite, Midianite, Sumerian, Assyrian, Hittite, Babylonian, Persian, and Roman Empires, and ALL of their **GODS** were left behind. Dream of Zion renewed was not left behind. All Jews underwent the wear and tear of conquest, destruction, and exile.
SOME JEWS HAD FORSAKEN GOD

Exiled from their homeland, all Jews prayed for spiritual redemption from the religious oppression of the Diaspora. All Jews who remained Jews found incessant forced conversions, persecutions, and pogroms throughout Western and Eastern Europe. Thirty-four expulsions were recorded: For 2000 years, Christian hatred of the Jews consumed. Many Jews died "Al Kiddush Hashem." Thousands upon thousands of Christians fought against the enemies of Christ. Thousands upon thousands of Muslims fought against the infidels: Christians vs. Muslims (to this very day) each take turns leaving each other behind...proselytes vs. apostates. **The Greatest Lie Ever Told in the Name of GOD** descended: The death of Jesus was good for Christians and bad for Jews. For Christians: **"Jesus Died for You, So You Can Live and You Get Eternal Life."** For Jews: **"Jesus Died and You Killed Him and You Get Premature Death."** Relationships of religion, resources, and revenue were familiar family lies. Many Jews witnessed verbal slanders turned into violent physical deeds.
ALL JEWS SAW THEIR FATE IN GOD'S HANDS

All Jews and only Jews were no longer given choices: economic discrimination, social ostracism, personal humiliation, and the **"THE FINAL SOLUTION."** Familiar family lies. The yellow star descended. Jews, cast as wandering exiles, were recast for genocide. Swastikas descended. Less than one fourth of one percent of the world's population were targeted for extermination. Shaved heads and tatooed numbers burned into arms descended. Many Jews were deported to concentration camps (human flesh burning crematoria, gas chambers, and hospital rooms for scientific experimentation): Zyklon-B gas was consumed. One third of worldwide Jewry was annilated. Six million sacred Jewish souls were left behind, their physical bodies exterminated, their seeds of immortality extinguished. A few Jews committed suicide on their way to, inside of, and soon after, the ominous death camps.

SOME JEWS LOST GOD

Homebound, all Jews wanted to go home. Some Jews had families and some Jews were orphans. All Jews were the children of God. Ascending, some Jews went to Canada; a few Jews went to South Africa where the world was divided into white on black; a few Jews went to Argentina with the escaped Nazis. The Jewish Brigade of Palestine was not consumed. The slogan, **"Jews Can Fight and Jews Can Win"** ascended. In the Pope's office, blaming the Jews for **DEICIDE** was left behind. UN Resolution 3379, Zionism was Racism, was left behind. Many Jews went to America with ALL worldwide refugees (to this very day). On the Statue of Liberty, Emma Lazarus's poetry ascended. Irving Berlin's compositions, "God Bless America" and "Israel" ascended. Ascending, the sexiest woman alive, Marilyn Monroe, converted to Judaism. In Sweden, Alfred Nobel, cast as a dynamite manufacturer, was recast as the good will manufacturer of Nobel Prizes. Jewish genius ascended and was recognized: For WORLD PEACE: Alfred H. Fried (1911); ... For ECONOMICS: Paul A. Samuelson (1970); ... For CHEMISTRY: Adolph Von Baeyer (1905);... For PHYSICS: Albert Abraham Michaelson (1907);... For MEDICINE and PHYSIOLOGY: Elie Metchnikoff (1908); ... Jews hold 20% of the Nobel Prizes. Jews wrote the popular Christmas songs: White Christmas, Rudolph, The Red-Nosed Reindeer, Let it Snow, Silver Bells, and Chestnuts Roasting on the Open Fire. Ascending, worldwide, humanity as a whole benefits from these magnificent, monumental, and momentous contributions from less than one fourth of one percent of the world's population. In 50 countries, Lubavitch-Chabad emissaries were left behind and not consumed: Jewish spiritual reinvigoration ascended. Many Jews witnessed a glimmer of the glorious face of **GOD**.

SOME JEWS SAW GOD EVERYWHERE

HOME SWEET HOME: Jews from every country in the world went home: Jews from 102 countries, speaking 82 languages ascended. On May 14, 1948, the vision of Theodor Herzl ascended: First as pioneers, then as soldiers and citizens, and finally as Zionists. The national anthem, **"Hatikvah,"** ascended. The Hebrew language ascended. Falafel in pita with tehina sauce was consumed. A miracle: "The Old Israel's" GOD YHWH was not consumed in the Holocaust. Triumphant, the Israel Defense Forces ascended. All Jews, cast as sacrificial lambs, were recast as sacrificial LIONS: Arab Riots and Revolts, War of Independence, Suez Canal, Six-Day War, Yom Kippur War, Lebanon War, Iraqi Scud Missile Crisis, and Incessent Terrorism descended. The Nation of Israel reborn was reckoned with, reconciled with, and was recognized by the world. Israeli operations resettled the exiles and unsettled the enemies. In this birthplace of ancient miracles, modern miracles of medicine, science, and technology ascended. Democracy ascended. The nomads of the desert were not consumed; civilization was not an oasis. The greetings, "Shalom Aleichem" among Jews and "Salam Aleikem" among Arabs acsended: "Baruch Hashem," and "Inshallah": an imperfect PEACE is ascending in an imperfect world, birthplace of the One and Only Perfect GOD. **The tri-part unity of the Jewish people, the Torah and the Biblical Homeland set a historical precedent.** God's promise of a land flowing with milk and honey is ascending: "Wherever Jews Go, Grass Grows; Wherever Israelis Go, Gardens Grow." This year of 5758 is the State of Israel's 50th Anniversary. The Jewish historical past was in the Diaspora; the historical future is in Israel. Some Jews born in Israel live everywhere... on temporary leave. **Israel is the only HOMELAND these Jews will ever know!**

MANY JEWS RECLAIMED GOD

POETRY WORLD RECORD

Bibical Eve is Given a Voice, and Liberated from 5000 Years of Misogyny

1. It is a Poetry World Record of 120 words of rhyme from one family of rhyme.
2. It is an unchallengeable literary feat by a woman never before done by a man.
3. Every single verse has poetry, philosophy, and comedy.
4. The poem travels a long distance, from the birth of Adam to the present moment.
5. I gave Eve, the first woman of the Bible a voice, and liberated her from 5000 years of mysogyny. **Someone had to do it!**
6. Philosophy: In each stanza, there is a **known** and **unknown**.
7. The structure of the poem follows the exact format of the verses from the Bible.

Genesis 2:18-23	
Genesis 2:16	Stanza One: Gift of Eve
Geneis 3:1-5	Stanza Two: Forbidden Fruit
Genesis 3:6	Stanza Three: Eve's Gift
Genesis 3:20	Stanza Four: Serpent
Genesis 3:6	Stanza Five: Adam Eats Fruit
Genesis 3-12	Stanza Six: Adam Blames Eve
Genesis 3:17-19	Stanza Seven: The Exile
Genesis 3:23	Stanza Eight: Eve's Gift of Childbirth
Genesis 3:16	Stanza Nine: Adam and Eve's Gift (SEX)
Genesis 4:1	Stanza Ten: Future Generations
Genesis 5:1	

120 Words of Rhyme From One Family of Rhyme

#1 Poetry Website for Student Projects

THE GREATEST POEM EVER WRITTEN ON EVE
POETRY WORLD RECORD
120 WORDS OF RHYME FROM ONE FAMILY OF RHYME
EVERY VERSE HAS POETRY, PHILOSOPHY, AND COMEDY
AN UNCHALLENGEABLE LITERARY FEAT BY A WOMAN
AN UNCHALLENGEABLE LITERARY FEAT FOR ALL EONS
POEMS TRAVELS FROM CREATION TO PRESENT MOMENT
EVE LIBERATED FROM 5000 YEARS OF MISOGYNY

Through the Eyes of Eve
GOD Gave Adam the Gift of Eve (Genesis 2:18);
GOD Gave Eve the Gift of Life (Genesis 2:20).

Foreshown
GOD **Knowingly** gave to Adam alone
the gift of **UNknown** Eve of clone
to be sewn from Adam's gift of bone
for his very own (Oy, a wishbone) (Genesis 2:18 - 23).

GOD spoke to Adam
about that **UNKnown**, forbidden tree of Knowledge of Good and Evil, full-grown, a **Known** safety zone (Oy, a danger zone of clingstones) (Genesis 2:16).

ForeKnown (Oy, tales without a tailbone)
good or bad, the serpent **Knowingly Knew**, that
Eve's interpretation of what GOD had said was matter of fact, untrue;
UNKnowingly, through the serpent's eyes, eating the fruit to Eve's surprise, would not be her demise (Oy, the matriarch known was not to be dethroned) (Genesis 3:1-5).

In the eyes of Eve,
outgrown, with a bigger breastbone (Oy, silicone)
ingrown, it was instinctively **Known, UNKnowingly** childbearing prone, that feeding and eating were good for Knowledge (Oy, gotta graduATE college) (Genesis 3:6),
as GOD **Knowingly** gave to Eve alone
the gift to be the she-bearer of the womb of life, as shown (Genesis 3:20).

In the eyes of Eve,
UNKnowingly naked … Adam ate
fruit **UNbeKnown** (Oy, a crazy bone), full of secrets, **Known** to be sacred
(Oy, bemoan, a kidney stone) and (Oy, begroan, a gallstone) (Genesis 3:6).

In the eyes of Adam,
on his own, his behavior **Known**, (Oy, a poor retinal cone)
Eve was **UNKnowingly** blamed (Oy, a jagged jawbone) and disowned,
Eve was on her own "sticks and stones may break my bones, but names… I married a doggone knucklebone" (Oy, a combat zone) (Genesis 3:12).

In the eyes of GOD,
Adam did not acKnowledge his **Known** misdeed
for a commandment intoned, that he had **Known**, and must atone,
(Oy, poor earphones), out of tune and out of tone, monotone, if only he had **KNOWN!**
OY, a CYCLONE of hailstones "fire and brimstones"; cause GOD has no funny bone (Genesis 3:17-19)
…**UNKnowingly** rezoned (Oy, an eroding ozone)
Adam tiller of the Garden of Eden (Oy, a tropical zone)
well Known is overthrown to till (Oy, my backbone),
the overblown soil of an overgrown windblown, grass-grown garden **UNKnown** (Oy, the grindstone):
fieldstone, sandstone, millstone, cobblestone, soapstone, drystone, ironstone, and limestone are RESEWN
with firestone and paving stone into capstone, cornerstone, copestone, curbstone, foundation stone, and brownstone,
OY, Adam's aching shoulder bone, hipbone, thighbone, knee bone, anklebone, chinbone, and shinbone (Oy, muscle tone) (Genesis 3:23).

GOD gave Eve
of her very own (Oy, Adam was outshone) the **Known** joyful gift of
a pubic bone, for **UNknown** painful childbirth, holding her own, groan, a milestone (Oy, phenobarbitone) (Genesis 3:16).

Adam and Eve gave to Each Other (Oy, hormones of progesterone and testosterone)
the **Known** cheekbone (Oy, seductive eau de cologne, and a gramophone playing a saxophone) of homegrown unforbidden immense sexual passion unchaperoned (OY, OY, ALONE) and
UNforeKnowingly, unforeseen orgasmic pleasures unforetold OY, OY, PHERO-MOANS (Genesis 4:1).
Enthroned, Adam gave Eve a **well Known** precious stone, a glistening gemstone, not made of
UNknown birthstone, cinnamon stone, moonstone, toadstone or rhinestone (Oy, a touchstone).

Adam and Eve gave GOD
Future Generations of **KNOWN** (Oy, a microphone) and **WELL KNOWN** (Oy, a megaphone) and
UNknown, no speakerphone or dialtone on the telephone or cellphone (Oy, postponed, Oy, Oy, Oy Vai Iz Mir!
"DUST to dust" gifts, a loan; and a gravestone [Oy, a tombstone of headstone or footstone?]
of **KNOWING** -a stepping stone- (Oy, a rosetta stone or philosophers' stone) and
unKnowing -on their own- (Oy, accident prone) (Genesis 5:1).

I gave Eve, the first woman in the Bible a **VOICE**, and liberated her from **5000** years of **MISOGYNY**.
Someone Had To Do It!

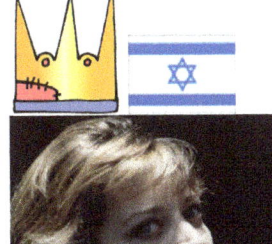

Sharon Esther Lampert
Sexiest Creative Genius in Human History
8th Prophetess of Israel: 22 Commandments
© All Rights Reserved.

www.PoetryJewels.com
Diamonds, Emeralds, Sapphires, Rubies, and Pearls

THE SOLE INTENTION OF MY POETRY IS TO ADD LIGHT TO YOUR SOUL

To Be Continued …

POETRY WORLD RECORD "Through the Eyes of Eve"
120 Words of Rhyme from One Family of Rhyme

Stanza One: Gift of Eve
1. foreshown
2. alone
3. unknown
4. clone
5. sewn
6. bone
7. own (kabbalistic significance)
8. wishbone (kabbalistic significance)

Stanza Two: Forbidden Fruit
9. full grown
10. known (kabbalistic significance)
11. safety zone
12. danger zone
13. clingstones

Stanza Three: Eve's Gift
14. foreknown
15. tailbone
another rhyme: knew, untrue
another rhyme: eyes, surprise, demise
16. dethroned

Stanza Four: Serpent
17. outgrown
18. breastbone (kabbalistic significance)
19. silicone
20. ingrown
21. prone
another rhyme: eating, feeding
another rhyme: knowledge, college
22. shown (kabbalistic significance)

Stanza Five: Adam Eats Fruit
another rhyme: naked, sacred
23. unbeknown
24. crazybone
25. bemoan
26. kidney stone
27. begroan
28. gallstone

Stanza Six: Adam Blames Eve
29. retinal cone
30. jawbone
31. disown
32. sticks and stones may break my bones
33. doggone (kabbalistic significance)
34. knucklebone
35. combat zone

Stanza Seven: The Exile
36. intoned
37. atone
38. earphone
39. tone
40. monotone (kabbalistic significance)
41. cyclone
42. hailstone
43. brimstone
44. funny bone
45. rezoned
46. ozone
47. tropical zone
48. well known
49. overthrown
50. backbone
51. overblown
52. overgrown
53. windblown
54. grass-grown
55. grindstone
56. fieldstone
57. sandstone
58. millstone
59. cobblestone
60. soapstone
61. drystone
62. ironstone
63. limestone
64. resewn
65. firestone
66. paving stone
67. capstone
68. cornerstone
69. copestone
70. curbstone
71. foundation stone
72. brownstone
73. shoulder bone
74. hipbone
75. thighbone
76. knee bone
77. anklebone
78. chinbone
79. shinbone
80. muscle tone

Stanza Eight:
Eve's Gift of Childbirth
81. outshone
82. pubic bone
83. groan
84. milestone
85. phenobarbitone

Stanza Nine:
Adam and Eve's Gift (SEX)
86. hormone
87. progesterone
88. testosterone
89. cheekbone
90. eau de cologne
91. gramophone
92. saxaphone
93. homegrown
94. unchaperoned
95. phero-moans
96. enthroned
97. precious stone
98. gemstone
99. birthstone
100. cinnamon stone
101. moonstone
102. toadstone
103. rhinestone
104. touchstone

Stanza Ten:
Future Generations
105. microphone
106. megaphone
107. speakerphone
108. dialtone
109. cellphone
110. telephone
111. postpone
112. loan
113. gravestone
114. tombstone
115. headstone
116. footstone
117. stepping stone
118. rosetta stone
119. philosopher' stone
120. accident prone

Philosophy Zone

Known and UnKnown

Stanza One: Adam's Gift of Eve
- **Known:** God
- Unknown: Eve

Stanza Two: Forbidden Fruit
- **Known:** Tree of Life
- Unknown: forbidden fruit

Stanza Three: Serpent
- **Known:** serpent
- Unknown: Eve

Stanza Four: God's Gift to Eve
- **Known:** God
- Unknown: childbearing

Stanza Five: Adam Eats Fruit
- **Known:** sacred secrets
- Unknown: fruit

Stanza Six: "Combat Zone"
- **Known:** Adam's behavior
- Unknown: Eve is blamed

Stanza Seven: The Exile
- Well Known: Garden of Eden
- **Known:** Commandment
- Unknown: Adam is rezoned

Stanza Eight: Eve's Gift
- **Known:** joyful children
- Unknown: painful childbirth

Stanza Nine: Adam and Eve's Gift
- **Known:** sexual passion
- Unknown: orgasmic pleasure
- Well Known: glistening gemstone
- Unknown: stones

Stanza Ten: Future Generations
- Well Known: megaphone
- **Known:** mircrophone
- Unknown: accident prone

Yiddish Translations:
Oy: interjection, denotes a negative emotion
Oy Vai Iz Mir: woe is me

Bible Zone: Dvar Torah
Princess Kadimah's Interpretation of Adam and Eve:
1. God creates the world and separates light from darkness, day from night, evening from morning, rivers from earth, sky, seasons, days and years.
2. God creates Adam and Eve, and they are living in the Garden of Eden or in **God's womb** and they are attached by **God's umbilical cord**, and God has to give birth to them (separate). When Eve eats the fruit, she has reached maturity, and it is time for God to give birth to Adam and Eve, to separate from them. Adam and Eve exit God's womb to serve God and continue the creation.

Poetry Review

"Through The Eyes of Eve"

A Poetic Classic, Deeply Philosophical, Eternally Feminine, Biblical & Modern, Melodious, Mystical, Scholarly and, Oh (Oy), So Very Humorous, **JUST DIVINE!"**
—E. Peters

---

1. Poetry segues into philosophy, comedy, and Biblical scholarship.

2. There is a universal message of **knowns** and **unknowns** for all people of all ages.

3. There is a reinterpretation of the text, the drama between Adam and Eve that finally sets Eve free from 5000 years of misogyny—Eve is now a liberated woman!

10 Poetry Reading Tips

1. Begin reading the poem to yourself silently.

2. Become familiar with the poem.

3. Read the poem by feeling and following the rhythm.

4. Take note of words needing emphasis.

5. Take note of places to pause.

6. Get to know the poem well.

7. Read the poem aloud in a natural voice.

8. Read the poem for surface meaning.

9. Reread the poem for the larger meaning of underlying ideas and depths of emotional power.

10. After reading the poem, reflect silently.

#1 Poetry Website for Student Projects

THE GREATEST POEM EVER WRITTEN ON CAIN AND ABEL
Cain's Mark: Inseparable, Together-Alone-Forever

Inseparable -
Cain and Abel were Born in the same Womb.
As Brothers like One. Together.
After Birth Separated Them into Two.
As Strangers like Enemies. Alone.

Inseparable -
Abel's Offering was Accepted by God. Together.
God Can. Together.
Cain's Offering was Rejected by God. Alone.
God Can't. Alone.
Cain Felt Humiliated as One. Alone.
Abel Can and Cain Can't.

Inseparable -
Cain and Abel were Left Alone Together.
Alone -
Cain was Left Able when Left Alone with Abel.
Alone -
Abel was Left Dis-Abled when Left Alone with Cain.
Abel Felt Cain's Humiliation as One. Alone.
Cain Can and Abel Can't.

Inseparable -
Abel was Left Dead - Rejected by God. Alone.
God Can't. Alone.
Cain was Kept Alive - Accepted by God. Together.
God Can. Together.
God Can and God Can't. Together.

Inseparable -
Together -
God Alone was Left Un-Able to **SAVE** the Lone Abel. Injustice.
Abel Can't and God Can't. Alone.
Together -
God Alone was Left Un-Able to **STOP** the Lone Cain. Injustice.
God Can't, Abel Can't, and Cain Can. Alone.

INSEPARABLE -
ALONE, CAIN CAN. Imperfected Imperfections of Perfection. **INJUSTICE.**
Together, The **PERFECT** God and The **PERFECT** Creation, Flawed. **INJUSTICE.**
Together with the Lone Cain, God **ALONE** was Left Humiliated. **INJUSTICE.**
God Can't and **CAIN CAN.** Alone.

Cain's Mark -
Together, a Conjoining of Cain's Crime and a
Constant Reminder of Abel's Reprehensible Murder.
Like Before Birth, As Brothers like One. Together.
Like After Birth, As Strangers like Enemies. Alone.
Inseparable, Cain was Left Together with Abel. Alone. Forever.

Sharon Esther Lampert
Sexiest Creative Genius in Human History
8th Prophetess of Israel: 22 Commandments
© All Rights Reserved.
www.PoetryJewels.com
Diamonds, Emeralds, Sapphires, Rubies, and Pearls

THE SOLE INTENTION OF MY POETRY IS TO ADD **LIGHT** TO YOUR SOUL.

#1 Poetry Website for Student Projects

POETRY IS AN ESSENTIAL SERVICE

www.WorldFamousPoems.com
The Greatest Poems Ever Written on Extraordinary World Events

Coronavirus: The World We Left Behind

PoetryEssentialService.com

(1) I had a very bad dream that haunted me all day. I woke up to a new world order. A virus had taken over the world, and declared itself the supreme leader.
Day Is Night, Night Is Day

(2) I am running out of breath as I breathe in the virus. I feel the muscle aches, my body is chilled to the bone. I can't stand up, I lie down. The lethargy is debilitating. I remember the face of the man who sneezed in front of me on the New Year's Eve boat ride. I could pick him out in a lineup.
Day Is Night, Night Is Day

Note:
Jan 1 2020 COVID19

June 2020 Anti-Body Test

(3) My soul speaks a final prayer as my body launches a final attack. Tissues catch bloody sputum. Antibodies rise up to destroy COVID19. A month of armed resistance with acidic gallons of vitamin C of fresh lemons. **PURmist Steam Inhaler** liberates my body, mind, and soul. **I WON!**
Day Is Night, Night Is Day

NOTES:
God's Wrath and Biblical Plagues:
1. Water to Blood: Ex. 7:14–24
2. Frogs: Ex. 7:25–8:15
3. Lice or gnats: Ex. 8:16-19
4. Wild animals or flies: Ex. 8:20-32
5. Pestilence of livestock: Ex. 9:1–7
6. Boils: Ex. 9:8–12
7. Thunderstorm hail & fire: Ex. 9:13–35
8. Locusts: Ex. 10:1–20
9. Darkness for three days: Ex. 10:21-29
10. Death of firstborn: Ex. 11:1–12:36

CDC Plagues 2020
- Tuberculosis, Bacteria
- Malaria, Parasite
- Measles, Virus
- HIV, Virus
- Polio, Virus
- Yellow Fever, Virus
- Tropical Diseases, Bacteria

NEW YORK CITY 2020
- April 8, 2020: #799 Dead
- Total Dead: #32,000
- July 13, 2020: **No Deaths!**
- N.Y. Governor Cuomo **Flattens Curve!**

(4) It is the first night of Passover **GOD'S WRATH:** Ten Biblical plagues pass over. It is another night of a **PANDEMIC.** One virus is passing over, striking all of us, yet killing the weakest among us. **#STAYHOME**
Global Catastrophic Trauma!
This Is why **God** Is not an **Essential Service!** The Deliverers: Moses and the Ten Commandments; and Dr. Fauci, and the Ten CDC Guidelines.
THE EXODUS: PASS THE MATZAH!
Offices! Schools! Stadiums! Restaurants!

(5) Civil rights are nullified: Mitigation is enforced. We are masked and muzzled. When I breathe into my mask, My glasses fog. I can't see! I can't talk! I can't sing! I can't smile! No selfies! We shelter in place together, but die **Alone** in the Emergency Room.
Day Is Night, Night Is Day

(6) Game On: Germ Warfare U.S.A. vs. COVID19
UNFAIR ADVANTAGES:
- Enemy Is an Invisible Mutating Monster
- Murderers Are Microbes Not Missiles!
- Viscious Cycle of Victim and Victimizer! Patricide, Matricide, Femicide, and Fraticide!
- We Murder Loved Ones—Not Enemies!

(7) **TOO LITTLE TOO LATE!** Bill Gates Sounded the Alarm! (YT, 2015)
Trump Speaks **TRUTH** to Woodward: **"This Is Deadly Stuff!"** (Jan. 28, 2020)
Trump Speaks **LIES** to American Public: **"This Is Just a Flu!"** (Functional Psychotic)
HOPELESS: President Trump's USA **PANDUMBIC** is the World's Worst Crisis.
HOPE: N.Y. Governor Andrew Cuomo **FLATTENS THE CURVE!** (July 13, 2020)

(8) **"THE TRUMP VIRUS"** The White House Flag is Lowered to Half Staff.
USA Fatalities: One Million Americans (2022) (4% of World, 20% of Cases)
Unmasked Anti-Vaxers Rejoice, **"God Will Protect Me!"** (Bag Em-Tag Em!)
Divine Intervention: **"God Helps Those Who Help Themselves!"**
A Silver Lining: 6-feet apart sounds like a **WORLD PEACE PLAN!**

(9) We **ZOOM** into our future. Halfsies: neckties & pajamas Children dare not go out and play. Lovers dare not meet, eat, and make love. We can only **DAYDREAM** of **THE WORLD WE LEFT BEHIND**

Sharon Esther's brain conceptualizes **BIG IDEAS** using one letter of alphabet:
- **CUPID:** Languages of Love —Written in Letter **C**
- **TEMPORARY INSANITY** —Written in Letter **S**
- **SECRET SAUCE** —Written in Letter **P**

NYU honored Sharon Esther with an award for "Multi-Interdisciplinary Studies" (on YouTube)

By Sharon Esther Lampert
www.SharonEstherLampert.com
FANS@sharonestherlampert.com
Prodigy: 10 Esoteric Laws of GENIUS
Prophet: 22 Universal Moral Compass
Philosopher: GOD TALKS TO ME: A Working Definition of God
Poet: World Famous Poems
Peacemaker: World Peace Equation
Paladin: SMARTGRADES BRAIN POWER REVOLUTION
Pin-Up: Swimsuit Calendar
Phoenix: Covid19 Antibody Superhero

LIFESAVER!
PURmist
Classic Steam Inhaler

NOAH FAN MAIL
FANS@SharonEstherLampert.com

Good afternoon to you. I am William. You are so freaking awesome I had to drop by and pay my respects and say hello.
Unreal set of accomplishments interests intelligence bright aura and brilliant mind all to go with one of the most beautiful women in this world.
All I can say is thanks for liking me it's a true privilege.
Blessings and prosperity to you.
—William

You seem to have a brilliant mind that's really possessing incredible depth. I'd love to learn from u.
—Alex

Sometimes you have to travel through a storm to find calm.
—Blaine K Taylor

Hi Sharon thank you for sharing. Now I know your intellectual side.
I can see significant literary and social awareness in your writing.
You would be an interesting person to converse with.
I also see a real spiritual side which is most important in today's secular world of confusion.
—Frank

Love it. Just woke up. But it is intriguing and joyous to hear from you and write to you. It says in Jeremiah that the very stars would fall from the sky before God ever were to forsake Israel.
Will write more, after my business day today.
You will be with me in my thoughts and prayers all day long today.
Shalom
—Herb

I love the new edition. Red white and blues. I like the Richard Branson reference. I don't know if it's insulting to Noah calling him a drunk ha! ha!
—Keith

Jewish New Year 5778

NOAH: Red or White? and the Blues

Hurricane Irma, Category 5, 185 Miles Per Hour Winds, AUGUST

1) This Rosh Hashanah is unlike any other: What did Noah do when the flood waters receded, and it was safe to step foot on dry land?

(2) What does a Rabbi do a week before the Jewish new year when the power is not on, Palm Beach Island is closed, half the traffic signals do not work (dangerous), and people are asked to stay home?

(3) God had promised not to destroy the world and Palm Beach Florida (read fine print in Midrash).

(4) God made a covenant with Noah; the first recorded "climate agreement" in human history entitled, "The Noahic Covenant or the Rainbow Covenant."

(5) A rainbow, called "My Bow," was given as the sign of a covenant "between me and you and every living creature with you, for perpetual generations" (9:2–17)

(6) Here comes IRMA: Floridians prepare for Armageddon the greatest hurricane to ever cross the Altantic ocean: Category 5, 185 miles per hour winds.

(7) Good idea: Send in a raven or a dove or send in the NOAA Hurricane Hunters who slice eye walls of howling winds, blinding rain, violent updrafts-downdrafts to enter the calm eye of the storm to take measurements.
(NOAA: National Oceanic and Atmospheric Administration)

(8) Ernest Hemingway's 52 polydactyly cats live in a feline fortress in the Keys— and do not evacuate:

(9) Sound familiar? After the flood, the Bible says that Noah drank wine made from this vinyard, and got drunk!
(Noah is the first alcoholic on Biblical record)

(10) Is Noah a good or bad role model? Billionaire Richard Branson defiantly refuses to evacuate, and survives Necker-Island hurricanes in his concrete underground wine cellar. Red or White?

(11) Red, white, and the blues: thousands of Americans became homeless and impoverished by 24-hours of raging rain, wicked wind, and malicious chutzpah.

- What happens when the ARK safety nets nets do not hold?
- How do you let go of yesterday?
- How do you start all over again from scratch?
- How do you create a fresh start?
- Where do you find support when every person around you is experiencing the same "stressor."

(12) This Rosh Hashanah is about celebrating a NEW YEAR 5778 and a BRAND NEW LIFE; for many in a new city; a new home; a new job; new friends; new neighbors; new temple
- One day at a time
- One foot in front of the other
- Focus on here and now
- Become the hero in someone else's life

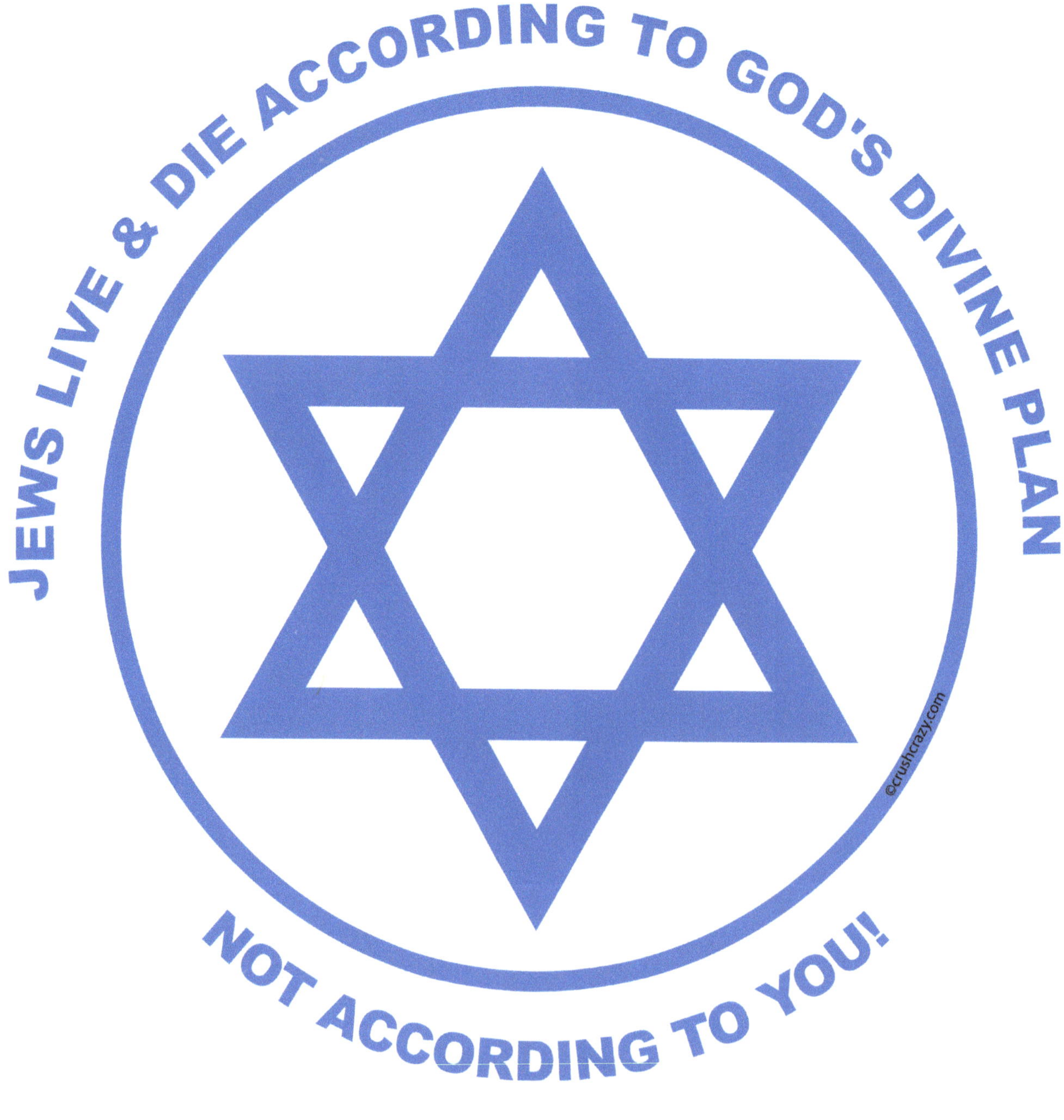
JEWS LIVE & DIE ACCORDING TO GOD'S DIVINE PLAN
NOT ACCORDING TO YOU!
©crushcrazy.com

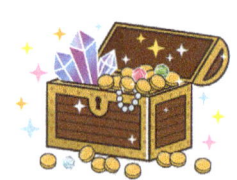

Performer: Sharon Esther Lampert
Israeli Day Parade Float
Every year, I march in the NYC Israeli Day Parade
I am the vocalist on the Jewish education float

Date: Thursday, November 19, 2009, 3:11 PM

Dear Ms. Lampert,
Hi
I am doing a poetry project for my English Honors 10th grade class and found your poem, "Simon Wiesenthal: Survivors Burden" and need the date of publication to include it in my project. I am also going to share it with my temple's confirmation class.

Thank you for getting back to me as soon as possible so I can finish my project.

Sincerely,
—Josh

So Special! A Letter from the Simon Wiesenthal Family

From: Joeri Kreisberg
Wednesday, March 29, 2006, 7:43 AM
Poem about Simon Wiesenthal

Dear Ms. Lampert,

I am in receipt of your letter to me with the poem written on my grandfather, Simon Wiesenthal.

First of all, apologies for my belated reply, which so late for various reasons, it has been quite a hectic time.

We were all very moved to receive the poem, and I made sure to distribute all copies thereof to my sister, Rachel and her husband Yossi and their three girls, Elah, Maya and Tali, to my brother Danny and his wife Orlee and their two children Liron and Shani, and of course to my wife Tamar, and our two boys David and Michael.

We very much appreciated your kind gesture, and I would like to thank you on behalf of all of us, including my parents, Paullina and Gerard Kreisberg.

All the best,
—Joeri Kreisberg
Ramat Gan 52521, Israel

THE SOLE INTENTION OF MY POETRY IS TO ADD **LIGHT** TO YOUR SOUL
THE GREATEST POEM EVER WRITTEN ON SIMON WIESENTHAL

A Memorial Tribute in Poetry to Simon Wiesenthal

A Survivor's Burden

After six million Jews were silenced:
Simon speaks above a hush.
Simon speaks above a whisper.
Simon speaks above an earshot.
Simon speaks out loud above the deafening scream of EVIL.

After six million Jews were silenced:
Simon's voice shatters the ghetto walls of anti-Semitism.
Simon's voice bellows in the streets of Argentina.
Simon's voice hallows in the halls of JUSTICE.
Simon's voice harkens in the International Arena of INJUSTICE.

After six million Jews were silenced:
Simon Wiesenthal WALKS his TALK and JUSTICE is done:
Adolf Eichman is brought to JUSTICE.
Franz Stangl is brought to JUSTICE.
Franz Murer is brought to JUSTICE.
Erich Rajakowitsch is brought to JUSTICE.
Hermine Braunsteiner is brought to JUSTICE.
Karl Silberbauer is brought to JUSTICE.
Josef Schwammberger is brought to JUSTICE.
1,100 Nazi War Criminals are brought to JUSTICE.

After six million Jews were silenced:
Simon Says:
"This man is on my list as a suspected war criminal."
Simon Says:
"When history looks back I want people to know the Nazis weren't able to kill millions of people and get away with it."
Simon Says:
"If we don't do anything about evil, that will encourage future perpetrators."
Simon Says:
"My work is a warning for the murderers of tomorrow."
Simon Says:
"Survival is a privilege which entails obligations. I am forever asking myself what I can do for those who have not survived."
Simon Says:
"I have received many honors in my lifetime; when I die, these honors will die with me, but the Simon Wiesenthal Center will live on as my legacy."
Simon Says:
"My epitaph should read simply **"SURVIVOR."**
Simon Says (in the afterlife... to the six million Jews murdered in the Holocaust):
"I didn't forget you."

Simon Wiesenthal (1908-2005)

On September 20th, 2005, Simon Wiesenthal died at the age of 96. He was born in the Ukraine. He was trained as an Architect. At age 36, he was liberated from the Mauthausen Concentration Camp. He had been imprisoned in a total of 12 concentration camps (five of which were death camps). He lost 88 relatives in the Holocaust. He married Cyla Muller, a survivor and had a daughter, Dr. Paulina Kreisberg: He has three grandchildren and seven greatgrandchildren. **He dedicated his life to tracking down, hunting, and gathering information on fugitive Nazis to bring them to justice for war crimes and crimes against humanity.**

He received many distinguished awards:
U.S. Congressional Gold Medal (1980)
French Legion of Honor (1986)
Presidential Medal of Freedom (2000)
Honorary British Knighthood (2004)
Austrian Golden Decoration of Merit (2005)

His memoirs and movies are entitled:
"I Hunted Eichmann" (1961)
"The Murderers Among Us" (1967)
"Justice, Not Vengeance: Recollections"(1989)
Academy Award-winning documentary, "Genocide"

Sharon Esther Lampert
Sexiest Creative Genius in Human History
8th Prophetess of Israel: 22 Commandments

www.PoetryJewels.com
Diamonds, Emeralds, Sapphires, Rubies, and Pearls

Todah Rabah to Karl, My Darling Muse
Written on October 6th, 2005
© All Rights Reserved

CHILD OF HOLOCAUST SURVIVOR'S BURDEN
I am a child of a Holocaust survivor...
The "Child of Holocaust Survivor's Burden" is to preserve the memories of the Holocaust survivor.
In this poem, I BEAR WITNESS to keep Simon Wiesenthal's message ALIVE for future generations.
I hope Simon Wiesenthal, the quintessential researcher, is proud of my ability to ferret out the facts of his life.

NOTES ON THE NAZIS:
Adolf Eichmann was a planner of Jewish extermination. Fritz Stangl was a commandant of two death camps. Franz Murer was "The Butcher of Wilno." Erich Rajakowitsch was in charge of the "death transports" in Holland. Gestapo officer Karl Silberbauer arrested Anne Frank in her Amsterdam hideout. Hermine Braunsteiner Ryan, helped process the murder of women and children at a camp in Poland and later was found living as a housewife in Queens, N.Y. SS Officer Josef Schwammberger used his German shepherd dog, Prince, to sadistically prey on Jewish inmates.

Edith Stein

Born a Jew, Became an Atheist, Converted to Catholicism Became a Nun,
Gassed at Austwitz as a Jew, and Beatified a Catholic Saint

Age: 51

1. October 12, 1891
   Edith Stein was born on in Breslau, Germany (now Wroclaw, Poland)
   Born into an Orthodox Jewish family

2. 1904, Edith Stein renounced her faith and became an atheist.

3. Student at the University of Gottingen, she received her doctorate in philosophy.
   She moved to the University of Freiburg, with Edmund Husserl and became his assistant.

4. Edith into contact with Roman Catholicism and read the autobiography of the mystic St. Theresa of Avila

5. January 1, 1922:
   Edith was baptized and taught at a Dominican girls' school in Speyer (1922 - 1932).
   She translated St Thomas Aquinas' De veritate (On Truth).

6. 1932-1933
   Edith became a lecturer at the Institute for Pedagogy at Munster
   Anti-semitic legislation passed by the Nazi government, forced her to resign the post in 1933.

7. 1934:
   Edith entered the Carmelite convent at Cologne, taking the religious name Teresa Benedicta of the Cross. She completed her metaphysical work 'Endliches undewiges Sein', an attempt to synthesize the diverse philosophies of Aquinas and Husserl.

8. 1938:
   Edith was transferred to the Carmelite convent at Echt in the Netherlands because of the Nazi threat. She wrote her important treatise 'Studie uber Joannes a Cruce: Kruezeswissenschaft'. Removing her from Germany, did not ensure her safety.

9. July 26, 1942:
   Adolf Hitler ordered the arrest of all non-Aryan Roman Catholics.
   Edith and her sister was seized by the Gestapo and shipped to the concentration camp at Auschwitz. Survivors of the death camp testified that she helped all other sufferers with great compassion.

10. August 9, 1942:
    Edith was sent to the gas chamber, where she died with her sister.

11. May 1, 1987:
    Edith was beatified by Pope John Paul II.

©EdithSteinFoundation.

#1 Poetry Website for Student Projects

THE GREATEST POEM EVER WRITTEN ON EDITH STEIN
CASTING LIGHT: Our sister, Edith Stein, of the Star of David; Their Sister, Teresia Benedicta, of the Cross

Spiritually at Unrest,
Our sister, Edith Stein recoiled into an atheist.
Her writings -forecast- a student of phenomenology; a PH.D. ascended.
Our sister, Edith Stein, of the Star of David, -cast- as an intellectual Jewess, -recast- herself
as their Sister, Teresia Benedicta of the Cross, a Roman Catholic, Carmelite Nun.

Physically at Unrest,
Once again -recast- as Edith Stein, of the Star of David, our sister, was -cast- down
into the gas chambers of Auschwitz; a yellow star was left behind.
Her Jewish identity, reconfigured into smoldering
ashes, was incontestable and unconsumable.
Life, in this world, was left behind.
All Jewish-born Catholic converts were consumed; baptism was left behind. Familiar family flaws.
Six million more Jewish souls were consumed. Silenced, eternally.
Relationships of religion, resources, and revenue were familiar family lies; baptisms by fire.
The prayers of their Sister, Teresia Benedicta, of the Cross were
-unheard- and -unanswered-

Physically and Spiritually at Unrest,
Edith Stein's Jewish identity, is -cast- back, twice,
EDITH STEIN -once- abandoned, in a concentration camp, ETERNAL DAMNATION;
EDITH STEIN -once again- forsaken, in a canonization council, DAMNED, ETERNALLY -

Once again -recast- as their Sister, Teresia Benedicta, of the Cross, our sister, Edith
Stein of the Star of David, -gassed- as one soul of the six million Jewish souls,
unable to save, secure, or salvage her own sacred soul, is -cast- up a heroic
savior, and is -recast- a saint for world-wide salvation.
Eternal life, ascended.
Their Sister, Teresia Benedicta, of the Cross, is -recast- as a Roman Catholic Martyr,
beatified in 1987, and canonized in 1998, by the Vatican, in Rome. Familiar family faith.
In between, on December 30th, 1993, the Vatican-Israel Accord was signed, and -cast- aside. Familiar family forgetfulness.
The memorial prayers, for our sister, Edith Stein, are recited on Holocaust Remembrance Day. Familiar family funeral and
folklore; Our Jewish people, eternally, living abroad in fear. Silenced.
Our sister, Edith Stein, of the Star of David, is -casting- light,
and ascending, as a Roman Catholic Saint.

Edith Stein

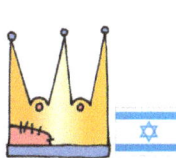

Benedicta McCarthy

Spiritually and Physically at Rest,
-Cast- adrift the soul of a two year old child, Benedicta McCarthy, is -cast- down
by a Tylenol overdose, is -cast- about by seizures, and is then -cast- up : THE MIRACLE.
Familiar family fact or fiction, faith or fantasy? fallacy? HEAVEN FORBID!
Our Dr. Ronald Kleinman is their credible witness. Familiar family friend or foe?
Life, in this world, ascended.
A single soul is not consumed.

The prayers, to their Sister, Teresia Benedicta, of the Cross, are **-heard- and -answered-**

Their Sister, Teresia Benedicta, of the Cross, is **-casting- light,**
and ascending, as a Roman Catholic Saint.

Physically at Unrest,
Their Eugenio Maria Giuseppe Giovanni Pacelli -cast- as a Reverend, was -recast- as Pope Pius XII:
The prayers, for the salvation of the soul of our sister, EDITH
STEIN, of the Star of David, -gassed- as one of the six million Jewish souls were
-unheard- and -unanswered-
Eternal Damnation.

Spiritually at Unrest,
Their Karol Joseph Wojtyla -cast- as a Reverend, is -recast- as Pope John Paul II:
The prayers, for the salvation of the soul of our sister, EDITH
STEIN, of the Star of David, who died a Jewess,
"Come Rosa, We Are Going For Our People,"* are
-unheard- and -unanswered- *N.Y.T., Oct. 11, 1998
Damned, Eternally.

Sharon Esther Lampert
Sexiest Creative Genius in Human History
8th Prophetess of Israel: 22 Commandments

www.PoetryJewels.com
Diamonds, Emeralds, Sapphires, Rubies, and Pearls

THE SOLE INTENTION OF MY POETRY IS TO ADD LIGHT TO YOUR SOUL

#1 Poetry Website for Student Projects

THE SOLE INTENTION OF MY POETRY IS TO ADD LIGHT TO YOUR SOUL.

This artwork is a reprint from a ceramic tile that I painted. The Holocaust Museum in Washington, D.C. sponsored a ceramic tile painting contest for children. Sutton Place Synagogue Hebrew School of N.Y.C. participated. I was a teacher in the afternoon Hebrew School and because I was not nine years old, I did not submit my tile for the museum exhibit. I am a child of a Holocaust survivor, and my tile was the only tile that depicted a Holocaust motif. I wrote "Divine Feathers of Sacred Freedoms" to accompany the ceramic tile that remained alone at the end of the art class and unbowed for the Washington Holocaust Museum. The tile is for the children who went through the Holocaust, and the poem is written in memory of the poets who perished in the camps or by suicide, during and after the Holocaust, such as: Stefan Zweig, Gertrude Kolmer, Nelly Sachs, Primo Levi, Paul Celan, Miklos Radnoti, Jerzy Kosinski, Arthur Koestler and Charlotte Solomon. Sharon Esther Lampert, © 1997.

Divine Feathers of Sacred Freedoms

Uprooted a Jewish Child Within Inner Walls of Outer Concentration Camp Barbed Wire Barely Survives.
Squeezing an Even Smaller Hand Broken by a Hard Lashing through an Even Smaller Opening in a Jagged Fence.
Opening the Filthy Palm of an Ever Weary Outstretched Arm to an Ever Watchful Majestic Bird Secure in a Deeply Rooted Tree.
Sharing the Sympathetic Bird Generously Lavishes Seven Magnificent Feathers of Flight Upon the Forsaken Child of Salty Tears.
Graciously by Divine Providence, All-Weathered Feathers Gently Descend, Spiraling Downward in a Fearless Fight for Freedom.
Sweetly: Laced by Soothing Tears of Dew Droplets... And Slowly: One by One by One... And Softly: Tenderly Touching the Thankful Palm.
Grasping Ever so Tightly All of the Frail Feathers of Forlorn Freedoms by Five Fragile Fingers Ever so Famished.
Imagining a Divine Grace, the Jewish Child Remembers, and Re-Attaches All Seven Feathers to Tattered Clothing on Shattered Bones.
Believing in a Brilliant Humanity of Eternal Divinity for the Jewish People, in Each Sacred Feather of Freedom:

1st Feather: **Israel**
2nd Feather: **God**
3rd Feather: **Torah**
4th Feather: **Prayer**
5th Feather: **Mitzvot**
6th Feather: **Self-Respect**
7th Feather: **Joy**

The Jewish Child Becomes Free.

Sharon Esther Lampert
Sexiest Creative Genius in Human History
www.PoetryJewels.com
Diamonds, Emeralds, Sapphires, Rubies, and Pearls
8th Prophetess of Israel (The 22 Commandments)
The Sole Intention of My Poetry is
to Add LIGHT to Your Soul.
Food is for the Body, Education is for the Mind,
and Poetry is for the Soul.

#1 Poetry Website for Student Projects

I made this flyer to distribute to educators across the state of Florida. In the heart of Boca Raton, Florida, one of the largest Jewish communities in th USA, the principal of the local high school was a Holocaust denier. The case is fascinating, as the community had to come together to fire him. Fascinating: Watch the YOUTUBE videos of the multiple trials and testimony.

Principal William Latson's BELIEVE IT OR NOT?
Spanish River High School Education System, Boca Raton, FL

BRD2

Jewish Community Is Outraged!

26 Years

Email Quote 1. "I Can't Say the Holocaust Is a Factual Historical Event!" — Principal William Latson

Email Quote 2. "Not Everyone Believes the Holocaust Happened!" — Principal William Latson

Email Quote 3. "I Do the Same with Information on SLAVERY!" — Principal William Latson

April 18, 2018

African American Community Is Outraged Too!

Holocaust Denial Is a Crime in 19 Countries
Germany 5 Years; Hungary 3 Years; Italy 6 Years

DADDY ABRAHAM LAMPERT
NICKNAME: BEZALEL

My Jewish Russian-refugee father was interned for 2 years in a Cyprus Detention Camp — Prime Minister Golda Meir visited. Shabbat Candelsticks are made of Cyprus Stone.
Exhibit: Museum of Jewish Heritage, NYC, November 15, 2000.
My father arrived in Israeli on a ship, "AF AL PI CHEN ("In Spite of Everything). The ship is in the Haifa Museum.

Exodus 31: 1-3

1. And the Lord spoke unto Moses, saying
2. See, I have called by name **Bezalel** the son of Uri, the son of Hur, of the tribe of Judah:
3. And I have filled him with the spirit of God, in wisdom, and in understanding and in knowledge, and in all manner of workmanship.

Reprinted in these Publications:

(1) The Orthodox Jewish Women's Renaissance Journal, December 1994, Kislev 5755, Vol.2, No.4, p. 18.

(2) Poem featured in Nate's Journ

(3) Poem featured in About.com Judaism website.

Resources of Healing for Children of Holocaust Survivors

(1) Children of the Holocaust by Helen Epstein

(2) Generations of the Holocaust by Martin S. Bergman and Milton E. Jucovy

(3) The Shadow of the Holocaust: The Second Generation & The Aftermath: Living with the Holocaust by Aaron Hass

(4) Memorial Candles: Children of the Holocaust by Dina Wardi

(5) Man's Search for Meaning by Victor E. Frankl

(6) Their Wounds by Marcus Rosenberg.

This poem is the poet's least favorite poem—yet poetry editors choose this poem to republish on their websites, in their newsletters, and in their magazines. SEL

My Father's Garden
An Eyewitness Account By a Child of a Holocaust Survivor

By Sharon Esther Lampert

My Father Labors In His Garden.
I am along side him. He is the only surviving member of his family as a result of the Holocaust. We are pulling out the weeds that have infiltrated the garden. The weeds are spreading out their roots and devouring the nutrients. The nutrients are needed by the flowers and vegetables that have begun to grow amidst the sandy earth and salty air inhabiting our home.

He Is Very Upset.
He is fiercely determined to rid himself of these weeds ... with a vengeance. Hoping to make a wish, I tear one weed from the grass and begin to blow on it, spreading its spores around the garden. "Don't do that," he screams, "That will only intensify the problem. The spores plant themselves in the soil and produce more and more weeds and jeopardize all the other plants in the garden."

He Is Always Screaming.
This is the way he communicates. It is an endless rage. The scream enters into me in a place where his communication has meaning. He has transmitted a message to me. I understand.

He Continues to Scream.
"To remove a weed from the garden you first plunge the knife into the soil surrounding the weed. Then position your hand firmly against the earth and rock the knife back and forth circling the weed to loosen the soil around its roots until the roots of the weed have nothing to adhere them to the earth." He Adds, "You Must Be Strong." I begin. He is alongside me. I grasp the knife. " It is a difficult task and you must not be afraid of the knife." he cautions. I plunge the knife into the soil . "Deeper," he says. "You must go deeper into the soil if you expect to reach the roots of the weed."

He Warns of Impending Doom.
"If you leave the roots of the weeds in the soil, then the time you have spent pulling out the weeds will be wasted. The roots will begin to grow and another weed will soon reappear."

He Has Experience.
I push the knife further into the ground, I am huffing and puffing. "Don't be scared of the knife." He hovers over me. "I'm not scared of the knife. I'm not strong enough to push it any further into the round." I reply.

He Reminds Me.
"I named you after my mother Sarah Esther and she was a very strong woman." My name is also representative of two very strong Jewish women in the Bible: Abraham's wife, Sarah, who had the chutzpah to laugh at God's will. And the beautiful Queen Esther who saved the Jews by marrying King Ahasvehrous to change his frame of mind about the fate of the Jewish people under his sovereignty. The message to safeguard Jewish life springs from a deep well of survival amidst adversity. The ethical transmission to safeguard life is paramount as I try to uproot this weed that has had the potential to destroy my father's garden and is always lifting its poisonous spores. The garden is the one place on the earth where he allows himself to be seen. He keeps to himself and to his garden. He is forever in hiding. He trusts no one.

He Places His Hand Over Mine.
His hand is twice the size of mine, hardened and very coarse. I can see, hear and feel his strength and resiliency penetrate the ground as the knife quickly slides deep down into the earth. This weed will have no future. He then twists and turns the knife around the roots keeping them intact so as not to break off their endings. The weed in its entirety is removed. My father's garden is free to flourish and to survive alongside of my father's wishes. The message that safeguards Jewish life - the fertilization of the seeds of life—has been transmitted.

NEW EXHIBIT: Opening November 15th, 2000

Museum of Jewish Heritage: A Living Memorial to the Holocaust
18 First Place, Battery Park City, New York, N.Y. 10004-1484
Info:(212)509-6130 • Tickets:(212)945-0039

Abraham Lampert
Cyprus Stone Shabbat Candlestick Sculptures

Sitting in a prison in Cyprus, my father, Abraham Lampert, sculpted these magnificent Shabbat candlesticks made of Cyprus stone. On November 15th, 2000, this extraordinary sculpture, and other well-crafted pieces of Cyprus stone are on exhibit at the Museum of Jewish Heritage in Battery Park, N.Y.C.

On display, there is also the original black-and-white photograph of my father sitting in prison and crafting this sculpture. This exhibit is only one of many other interesting exhibits that document the lives of Jews in the Cyprus Refugee Camp.

After the Holocaust, my father was the sole survivor of his immediate family; his mother, father, two sisters, their husbands and children were shot and buried in mass graves.

In hiding on foot, my father fled from country to country, and was imprisoned in Russia and released, and later imprisoned in Italy and released, and then by divine grace, boarded an illegal ship to Palestine called, "AF AL PI CHEN (In Spite of Everything)." Pictures of this Jewish refugee ship are on display in the Haifa Museum I spent quite a few hours looking for my father's face in those photos; but to no avail, however, on all return trips, I will try again.

I remember well these words told to me by my father, "I am the sole survivor of genocide, and as a Jew living in other peoples' lands, I cannot fight for what does not belong to me."

When enemies rise up against the Jews, they pack up their bags, and follow the EXIT signs when given the ultimatum of conversion or exile, or death. Tragically, in Europe, for 2000 years, this horrific reality tainted the lives of every Jewish family.

"After the Holocaust, I went to live in Israel and not America, Australia, or Canada, because in Israel, I have the RIGHT to FIGHT for what BELONGS TO ME: THE LAND of ISRAEL IS MY HOMELAND."

In 1947, the illegal refugee ship was on its way to Palestine and was intercepted by the British, 200 miles off the coast of Haifa. Captured, my father was sent to the Cyprus Detention Camp, where he was again imprisoned for a year and a half.

According to my father's recollections, Golda Meir did visit the prison and no, he did not ask her for her autograph, "She was a very busy lady, and did not have the time for such trivialities!"

In 1948, when Israel was declared a state, my father was released from prison. By divine grace, these sculptures, without a nick or a scratch, survived the arduous journey from the Cyprus camp, housing thousands of homeless Jewish refugees to Israel, the eternal Jewish homeland; as worldwide, a collective divine grace was granted for all Jewish people. 2000 years of Jewish exile had ended for all Jews; Baruch Hashem, GOD, the Torah, the Jewish people and the Land of Israel are reunited forever.

Alive, and in his senior years, fortuitously, my father is able to SEE with his one remaining eye, that is 80% blind, because of the crippling eye disease glaucoma, his Cyprus stone Shabbat candlesticks sitting on a beautiful pedestal in a museum display case, safe and sound, as his glorious divinely graced artistic gifts, enjoy the world's recognition and acclaim.

Baruch Hashem, these Cyprus stone Shabbat candlesticks flicker with immortality, for all future generations of Jews to cherish, as well as, for new Jewish sculptors to emulate; a small miracle of monumental divine proportions.

By Sharon Esther Lampert
Poet, Philosopher, Prophet and Princess, http://www.poetryjewels.com

Note: My father lived in Israel until 1948- 1960, in Bat Galim, Haifa, Israel.

Memorial Poems

In Memory

Rabbi Shlomo Carlebach

Santified Every Waking Moment
With his Joyous Singing,
Affectionate Loving Demeanor
And Wise Words of Torah;
Words of Torah that Reached
Up to Touch the Stars of
The Shabbat Evening Sky
Illuminating the Darkest Night
Bringing the Hope of Tomorrow's Dawn
Breaking Through and Shining Forth
Echoing Love, Peace, Respect, Harmony, and Joy
For ALL the Jewish People and
For ALL the Peoples on the Earth

SHABBAT SHALOM

#1 Poetry Website for Student Projects

July 11-July 13, 2011

The Murder of Leiby Kletzky

Abduction, Seduction, Destruction, Reduction, Construction, Deduction

HERO
Yaakov German
150 Shomrim
5000 Volunteers
Found Leiby
on Video
Camera

Seven blocks from home
when you are a big boy, age 8 and
your birthday is right around the corner
how scary can it be to walk home alone?

Leiby's neighbors are of his own kind
ultra-orthodox Jews:
**Bobov, Belz, Ger, Satmar, Stolin, Vizhnitz,
Munkacz, Spinka, Klausenburg, Skver, and Puppa**
Bearded men with dangling curls
in tall black hats and long flowing coats
The women are sporting glamorous wigs,
God-given children, and glatt-kosher groceries
Borough Park is the safest neighborhood in New York City

"THE BUTCHER OF BROOKLYN"
Levi is not one of them, he is an orthodox Jew
Levi is not one of them, but one of us, an outsider

We are all ashamed, humiliated, and heartbroken
We are all blinded by ignorance

Two-lost boys lost their lives:
Two Jewish boys, Leiby and Levi, share the same name
Leiby broke our hearts and Levi hardened our hearts

10,000 mourners mobilize for a funeral
Jews and Gentiles unite for justice for Leiby

Even incarcerated prisoners unite for justice for Leiby
Sane or insane, Levi deserves the death penalty

Levi Aron
40 Years to Life

One lost boy, Leiby, will have a law named in his memory
"Leiby's Law" to support surveillance cameras

Leiby, Amber, Etan, and Caley's memory rescues lost children:
- May 25: National Missing Children's Day for **Etan Patz**
- AMBER ALERT for **Amber Rene Hagerman**
- The Child Protection and Safety Act for **Adam Walsh**
- **Caylee's Law:** Failure to report a missing or dead child within 24 hours
- **Jaycee Lee Dugard** Foundation: Held captive 18 years, with 2 kids
- **Elizabeth Smart** Foundation: Raped 4-times a day

Leiby is no longer alone, lonely, or lost
Leiby found his voice and destiny

#1 Poetry Website for Student Projects

#EyalGiladNaftali July 10, 2014

#BringBackAllOurBoys
Eyal Yifrach, Gil-ad Shaar, and Naftali Fraenkel

There's an **APP** for that!
RED ALERT for terrorist!
Rockets, mortars or missiles into the State of Israel

ISRAEL: Why mess around in the land of the one **GOD**,
and the 3 **P**rophets: **M**oses, **J**esus, and **M**ohammed?

God is only found in a prayerbook
God is never found on the front page of a daily newspaper

Operation Brother's Keeper

Three Yeshiva boys murdered in retaliation for
Who knows what? Turn over every stone...

Landau said look for something that has been disturbed
Something unatural... rocks with muddy side facing up
Leaves of a bush with the waxy side facing down...

Seized on June 12; Bodies found June 30
Eyal Yifrach, Gil-ad Shaar, and Naftali Fraenkel
North of Hebron, Palestinian village of Halhul

Three unarmed Yeshiva boys returning
home after late night prayer study get into
a car with strangers at a hitchhiking point

This a tragedy waiting to happen **EVERYWHERE**:
Unarmed, hitchhiking, night, strangers — and HAMAS

At its worst, its an escalation of a war
on a 60-year old battlefield with **HAMAS**

Pay attention to 3 red flags: **A**nyone! **A**nywhere! **A**nytime!
ALL EVIL IS JUSTIFIED!

Jewish Hostages in Texas, January 15 2022

RUN SAID RABBI

A cup of tea
A slice of pizza
A can of soda
A chair
A British national
An Islamic meshuganah
A Pakistani anti-Semite
A lone-wolf psychopath
Malik travels 5000 miles
Takes four Jewish hostages
In the state of Texas
At Beth Israel, Colleyville
FBI negotiations: 11 hours
Meshuganah said: "Get on your knees!"
Rabbi Charlie Cytron-Walker said: "No!"
We were not freed or rescued
We escaped inching towards
the exit door as meshuganah
put gun down to sip on his soda
Rabbi threw chair
Rabbi said: "**Run!**"
L'Chaim!
FBI fired all bullets.
One less meshuganah in world
Today feels lighter and brighter!
LChaim!

"The Sole Intention of My Poetry Is to Add LIGHT to Your Soul"
Sharon Esther Lampert

"Food Is for the Body Education Is for the Mind Poetry Is for the Soul"
Sharon Esther Lampert

"Every Thought in Your Head was Put There by a Writer"
Sharon Esther Lampert

LITERATURE Is Powerful Beyond **WORDS** For It Creates **WORLDS**"
Sharon Esther Lampert

Sharon Esther Lampert
First Responder Poet
www.SharonEstherLampert.com
One of World's Greatest Poets

FAN MAIL
FANS@SharonEstherLampert.com

Well they are beautiful poems and wonderful writings.
I did go to poetry jewels today, but I confess, mainly to look at your legs.
Shabbat Shalom.
—Bernstein

Dear Princess Kadimah:
Thank you for putting your poetry on the net, especially the one about dating an Israeli man. It helped me sort out a date I had Saturday with an Israeli (former military soldier, of course). Jewish guys always lunge at me, but this one was more like a missile. I don't know where to file this experience.
Thanks,
—Kim

Sharon ("Kadimah"),
I just visited your website. Amazing! Your work is profound, prolific, and so beautifully poetic. Your beautiful and gentle soul seems so transparent through your writings. Your intellect abounds. I would love to know more...
I'd love to hear from you.
Warmly,
—David

... Moves me deeply. It's so rare to see such a physically beautiful, and spiritually profound, person on the net.
—AH Aaron Henry

December, 22, 2000
Thank you for letting me know of your poem. Edith Stein was a great and important person and it is good to know that she is being heard again.
—Paul

Paul Douglas Stamm
Technology Coordinator
Divine Savior Holy Angels High School
4257 N. 100th Street
Milwaukee, WI 53222
www.dsha.k12.wi.us

For My Love, A.K., American, Child of Holocaust Survivors from Poland

Rabbi Ari Intimate Blessings

Descending from a long line of orthodox rabbis—the orthodox rabbi appeared
I was an afternoon-conservative Hebrew-school teacher, popular and dear

We were both children of a Holocaust survivor, unconscious common ground
He was also a therapist, and poking around in my mind, he found
in my philosophical attitude and approach to life, a familiar-haunting sound

Models date rock stars; actresses date producers; athletes date cheerleaders;

Bosses date secretaries; chefs date waitresses; writers date editors;

Doctors date nurses; dentists date hygienists; therapists date patients;

Pilots date flight attendants; professors date students; sculptors date their nudes;

Nuns don't date their priests; **rabbis do date their Hebrew-school teachers**.

A boyfriend, I don't remember, a lover he became
I wasn't emotionally able to play the marriage game

Only one memory lingers of the covert love affair:
Making love and being wrapped tightly in his arms, is all I can recall
And where he put his key, he didn't carry on Shabbat, a crevice is in the wall

I feel infinitely blessed by the long lineage of rabbis in this very intimate setting
Blessings were given, all night long, even if there wasn't going to be a wedding

I can't recall how the love affair ended, a season at most, it is a mystery, oh dear...
Passions were set aflame and passions were requited in love.

He then set me **free**, and let me be **me**...
Ethereal: a celestial being, an angel, from way up **above**.

—Sharon Esther Lampert
March 3rd, 2004
Special Note of Gratitude to Rabbi Ari, My Muse

#1 Poetry Website for Student Projects

For My Love, Dr. K.C.

FIRST LOVE — SEE THE WORLD THROUGH THE EYES OF A CREATIVE GENIUS

As a college freshman, I was relentlessly pursued by an Italian-Catholic boy.

He asked me out to a movie:
I told him I couldn't go because "I AM JEWISH!"
He asked me where I was from: I said, "I AM JEWISH!"
He asked me what my major was: I said, "I AM JEWISH!"
He asked me what I wanted to be when I grow up – I mean graduated!
I said, "I AM JEWISH!"

For three months, he placed love notes into my dorm-room mailbox.
I still have them.

"With love's light wings did I o'er-perch these walls, for stony limits cannot hold love out," said Romeo.

He was brilliant, a Presidential scholar.
He was gorgeous, a member of the basketball team
He came from an all-boys Catholic high school;
I came from a Solomon Schecter Day School.
He said he wanted to convert.

What did he see in me? I had a mouth full of metal braces.
He gave me a button that said, "Tin-Grin." I have that too!

Love notes and all, he became irresistible:
The last image I remember before I got very lost in the throes of ecstasy
was of a wooden statue of JESUS hanging over his bed.
We were all naked.
Two of us were Jews.
Him, Me, JESUS: a Holy Trinity.
He had made me a woman.

Later, I was very miserable over the fact that I was so happy.

"I AM JEWISH...WOMAN!"

The nouveau Romeo & Juliet had met each other's parents too!

3 out of 4 parents wished them well—the 4th parent was a Jewish-Holocaust survivor.

"O happy dagger! This is thy sheath; there rust, and let me die," said Juliet.

When he grew up – I mean graduated! – he became, "A Nice-Catholic Doctor"... a Psychiatrist.

I was his first patient! — Parting is Such Sweet Sorrow, said Juliet.

"For never was a story of more woe than this of Juliet and her Romeo,"
said, William Shakespeare.

"Tin Grin" Sharon Esther Lampert
One of the World's Greatest Poets

For My Love, Y.J. Jacks, Israeli-Englishman

THAT KISS

Fortune teller that I AM,
My crystal ball sees ALL.
Clairvoyant, the man's libido is flam**BOY**ant.
I SEE: **ANIMAL MAGNETISM.**
Inside of **THAT KISS** will be BLISS.

Taking chances with amorous glances,
He advances... Lips pouting-tongue tied:
THAT KISS: SmOOch; smOOch.
When he romances: his gait prances,
His penis lances, his generosity enhances.
VOODOO, or DOO-YOU want dinner, dear?"
His heart dances....

Magician that **HE IS**,
He has a loaded deck of cards,
And wants to be my bodyguard.
Enchantment: a bag of mesmerizing tricks,
An **ACE** up his sleeve, a **KING** or a **JACK**
Are inside of his top hat of black.
Sleight of hand, **THAT KISS** is grand.

WIZARDRY: Pressed into his bosom,
I am caught in his embraces, arms
Flailing, like a net above my head,
His pounding heart is beating red.
THAT KISS tells **ALL** or just enough
To keep me Interested in **ALL** of his stuff.

Lips full of feelings, **THAT KISS**,
Soft as rose petals, free of prickly thorns.
In the the dark recesses of his mouth,
I find my way by the light in his eyes,
His smile is real, there is no disguise.

Even though we just met,
I am caught in the tangled web of
A hot-blooded, Israeli-Englishman:
"A Jack of All of Love's Trades."
A rare mixed-breed, a British accent,
Concealing a *Sabra, wherever he went.
Tricks of my own trade, I roll up my sleeve,
And I become a woman-in-need(?)
THAT KISS I can't forget, and with no regret:
It is almost 4 a.m., and inside of my gypsy's tent:
Sm(**OO**)ch, sm(**OO**)ch,
We are still one silhouette.

ANIMAL MAGNETISM:
Sm(**OO**)ch, sm(**OO**)ch,
Some call it v(**OO**)d(**OO**),
Most think it witchcraft,
Experts refer to it as "osculation."
Others call **THAT KISS** Kabbalah;
A kind of Jewish mysticism:
Many are in need of exorcism.

Translation: "Sabra" is a Jew born in Israel.

Sharon Esther Lampert
Sexiest Creative Genius in Human History
8th Prophetess of Israel: 22 Commandments
Todah Rabah to My Darling Muse Y.J. Jacks
© January 2003, All Rights Reserved.

www.PoetryJewels.com
Diamonds, Emeralds, Sapphires, Rubies, and Pearls

For My Love, Dr. J.P.M., Harvard M.D.
Parents: Half Jewish Holocaust Poland, Israel, N.Y. — Half-Arab Lebanese

My Man

Making Love All Through the Night
and Making Love All Through the Day

My Man
is passionate and strong, all through
the night—I know his emotional,
spiritual, and physical being; I feel
the breadth and depth of his masculinity

All through the night, **My Man** holds
me tightly in his arms: warm, tender,
and cuddly—childlike—always knowing
where I am, secure forevermore

My Man's touch lingers—
I am sleeping soundly all
through the night, still making
love with him, in my dreams

I awaken to **My Man's** soft kisses at
dawn, my spirit floating in the morning
mist—the promise of love is fulfilled—
my heart is murmuring a melody, a
sweet new song, all through the day

By Sharon Esther Lampert

@All Rights Reserved. Sharon Esther Lampert.

For My Love, Sivon, Israeli-New Yorker

Sivan Melody of F/Light

Dancing in his kitchen
To Cuban beats on a drum
Clothing falls to the floor, and
He sweeps me into the next door.

Making love in his arms
To Israeli rhythms on a heartbeat
Blankets fall to the floor, and
Passions are set free to pour.

Into the next day, as the music of
Love continues to play, a lovebird
Sitting on his sill, sings and sways, and
Waits for me to begin my day…

A cozy nest, a brief respite,
Before we again take flight,
Another day, another journey,
Encircling the sun, into the light.

Sharon Esther Lampert
Sexiest Creative Genius in Human History

Todah Rabah (Thank you) to Sivon,
My Darling Muse. A Gift of Immortality:
May You Live Forever in a Poem.

www.PoetryJewels.com
Diamonds, Emeralds, Sapphires, Rubies, and Pearls

Poetry Book: SWEET NOTHINGS

For My Love, Dr. Marc, Jewish American

Marc Speed of Light

My delicate hands are tucked securely
Into his manly palms; at the
Speed of light, I am melting into
His amourous outstretched arms.

Our eyes make contact, and
We are locked into a soft steady gaze.
The world is spinning around
Us, without ever a faze.
Our hearts are intertwining
In public view; and a man
Driving by yells out,
"Get a room!."

The mating dance has us both
Deep within it's magnetic grip:
He has kissed me a thousand times,
We are the movie within the movie,
In the fabulous "Seabiscuit" flick.
He is the leading man of my evening:
6'3, a pediatric an·es·the·si·ol·o·gist.
Built like Judah Maccabee:
A classic: tall, dark, and handsome,
Worthy of a King's ransom.

Sucking on Dylan's fanciful chewy candies,
Drenched in sugar, our kisses grow sweeter,
Our entangled tongues are drunk on love:
An auspicious day, chemistry is a gift
From the Gods, from way up above.

Deeply felt kisses penetrate,
The light in our souls radiate,
Baby, Baby, Baby: Here I am.
Honey, Honey, Honey: Yes you can.
Oh doctor, I hope you make house calls.
No hesitation for consummation,
Our bodies hunger for salvation.

Sharon Esther Lampert
September 14th, 2003

For My Love, Rodolfo, Jewish-South American, Uruguay

Rodolfo:
The Music, the Muse, and the Mystic

(I) Daydreaming:
In the synagogue, on the Sabbath,
He appeared: his face and body chiseled by
The hand of Michelangelo's "David."
On his tongue danced Yiddish melodies and
Meditations of Osho, the mystic;
In his hands, a a tennis racquet served up aces;
And in his eyes, an Angel was present,
Singing Hebrew prayers into his ears
As she beckoned and beseeched him to love.

(II) Daydreaming:
He flew north, away from the cold winter
In Uruguay, to warm his frozen heart
By the fireplace at her bed,
As the music of Vivaldi
Played on his mind and
Passionate patter recited in Spanish
Poured out from his machismo.
Caressing the sinewy
Wingtips of the Angel,
His spirit was longing for shelter
Beneath her ample wingspan.

(III) Daydreaming:
He had passed through 22
incarnations and was searching...
For room, board, and shelter, wanting
To be reincarnated as a foreign
College student in New York.
Piled high, tests, applications, and deadlines
Consumed his every wakeful moment.

(IV) Daydreaming:
Spent like Jacob, he began to wrestle with
The Angel, over a bowl of gazpacho,
Challenging her to confront the issues:
1. Does GOD Exist?
2. What is EVIL?
3. What is Anti-semitism?
4. Is there an Afterlife?
5. Did the Red Sea Part?
6. Did Moses Receive the Ten Commandments?
7. Are Jews the Chosen People?

V) Daydreaming:
The Angel, chopping on spinach salad, like popeye,
Answered -- in between each bite -- each and every
Paramount question posed that plagued her muse:

1. Does GOD Exist?
There is a power greater than you that exists in the world. To know GOD
Is to respect creativity and the infinite diversity of all creation.

2. What is EVIL?
People are NOT so EVIL, as they are SO STUPID.
Human Beings are the dumbest animals on the planet:
The rest of creation does not need therapy, mental institutions, or prisons.
GOD gave the animals twice as much and to live,
They don't have to work half as hard to survive:
Superior vision, hearing, and smell; and underneath
The fabulous-warm fur, my cat looks exactly like you.
A teeny-weeny ant lives in a complex civilization
And is smarter than an "average" human being;
An arctic polar bear can swim a thousand
Miles without a swimming lesson.
Even if human beings overcome their ignorance
They will never overcome their stupidity;
People go into education; but
The education does not go into them;
People go into religion, but
The religion does not go into them;
People go into love, but
The love does not go into them.
Every person has emotional problems and is his own worst enemy.
EVIL IS INSANITY: The world is NOT divided into
White vs. Black, Jew vs. Arab, Muslim vs. Christian, or Men vs. Women;
It is really divided along the lines of the SANE vs. the INSANE.
The sane choose **LIFE** and create and let live; the insane
Choose **DEATH** and destroy and build graveyards of hatred:
**BIG DICKS KNOW HOW TO BUILD SOMETHING and
Small dicks know how to destroy everything.**
"Pissed Off and Pissed Away" is the maxim muttered by small dicks.
THE ETERNAL PARADOX is Question 8: Why is it that the men with no dicks
(the cowards) are the men that become the dicks (the bullies)?
Most people do not have to look outside of one's own family to find **HATRED**.
Most people do not have enough **LOVE** inside of themselves to do what
they need to do for themselves.

3. What is Anti-semitism?
Q: Why is the **DEATH** of Jesus **GOOD** for Christians and **BAD** for Jews?
Christians are rewarded with eternal life:
"Jesus Died for You, So You Can Live."
Jews are punished with 2000 years of persecution and genocide:
**"Jesus Died Not For You; The Jews Killed Him.
THIS IS THE BIGGEST LIE EVER TOLD IN THE NAME OF GOD.**

4. Is there an Afterlife? When I walk, I step on the ants, and after I am
Dead, the ants will crawl on top of me.

5. Did the Red Sea Part? The physical splitting of the Red Sea is a
Metaphor for a greater spiritual reality: a crossing over from slavery to freedom.

6. Did Moses Receive the Ten Commandments?
Moses received the Ten Commandments, similar to Mozart
Who received a divine gift of music to be shared with the world.

7. Are Jews the Chosen People? The Jews chose to follow the Ten
Commandments of GOD as revealed in the Torah, the Five Books of Moses.

(VI) Daydreaming:
Rodolfo was on one of his many sojourns, in flight, north, south, east, and
West of Fifth Avenue, and in fright, with ten nail-bitten fingertips;
And the CDs of Best-loved Tchaikovsky fell into his hands, and he gifted
The entire collection to his best-loved Angel who taught him a few things.

(VII) Daydreaming:
Seven days and seven nights pass.
Eternal, the Sabbath returns to the synagogue.
Rodolfo Goldman, the muse, is now... **IMMORTAL:**
-- transformed by a mere transcription of the poet's pen --
On the eighth day, Rodolfo returns to Uruguay in brand new tennis sneakers.
In his hand is a poem entitled, "Rodolfo: The Music, The Muse, and The Mystic."
People from every corner of the world enter the "Rodolfo Poetry Contest,"
With NO FEE and NO DEADLINE ... And the Angel is left pondering the...
Immortal meditations of Osho, the mystic, as the
Immortal music of Vivaldi and Tchaikovsky, and the
Eternal questions play on and on and on and on and on and on and on...
And on.

www.PoetryJewels.com
Diamonds, Emeralds, Sapphires, Rubies, and Pearls

BY Sharon Esther Lampert
Sexiest Creative Genius in Human History

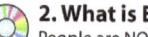

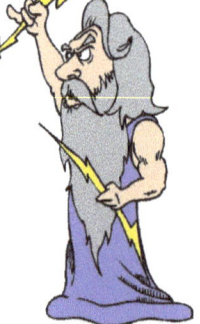

#1 Poetry Website for Student Projects

For My Love, Ziv, Israeli - Student in USA - Lives in Israel

Ziv Ha-schechina (rhyme)

From Jerusalem he came from above
On the glorious wings of a white dove.

His towering blue-eyed poetic playmate,
Was full of rhyme, and Philosophical discourse:
A grand date from the hand of fate.

With his new playmate in hand,
Life in New York was quite grand:
It all began with the Guggenheim,
Broadway, and Mozart:
Then they feasted on a Fudge Napoleon,
Profiteroles, and a Ricotta Cheese Tart.

Serenaded by a piano playing orange cat,
His pockets full of Jewish poetry grew fat.

Underneath oriental lanterns of starlight,
Friends from Australia chatted until twilight.

With bouquets of beautiful flowers in caverns,
It all ended with a splendid dance at Tavern.

On the wings of the white dove,
His face bearing the kisses of love,
With memories of embraces untold,
He returned to Jerusalem of Gold.

Sharon Esther Lampert
August 27th, 2003

For My Love, Yossi, Israeli, Sephardic—Tunisian

YOSSI: THE TOW TRUCK (rhyme)

Black diamond eyes, straight black hair,
Short, sexy, and virile, without ever a care.

Around his neck, a Magen David of gold,
His sexual escapades began at 13, if ever told.

A single red rose is in his outstretched hand,
Women of every persuasion are at his command.

From the Israeli army, he is a man in flight,
He appears on every other cold-winter night.

From way up above, he is ready for love,
At 22, in his sexual prime, he is all mine.

Lovemaking ends, and he transforms my rear into a drum,
From Tunisia, he is full of spirited joy, and begins to hum.

On my rear, he taps out a popular-Sephardic tune,
And sings along by the light of the shimmering moon.

He has produced a record, and presents me with a gift,
We sing a duet, and drift off into melodies with a rift.

He was the baby in his family, the **10th** and very-last child.
I am the first born of my family, the very opposite of wild.

During the day, he drives his own black-tow truck,
At midnight, his penis is in first gear, ready to fuck.

By Sharon Esther Lampert

For My Love, Gabriel, Israeli, Sephardic—Persian — American

GABRIEL: LOVER MAN RHYME

The Jewish New Year begins with the blast of a resounding shofar.
In a gold Lexus, a Persian jeweler is speeding across town in his car.

Direct, from Great Neck to Manhattan, he has traveled many miles,
Toting a bottle of whiskey and a can of coke, he wears only a smile.

Years prior, on Shabbat afternoons, a rendezvous for afternoon delight.
Years later, a memory lingering, brings him back again at twilight.

From his cell phone, he whispers a sweet nothing into my ear and makes a
request: sexy lingerie: red, pink, baby blue, purple, black or white is best.

He must smoke one cigarette, and I send him out into the lonely hall.
He must have his drink by his side, and sets up a table that won't fall.

My big-male orange cat sharing his pillow is a cross-cultural taboo.
He wants a new pillowcase to put him back into a romantic mood.

I turn on some soothing music and light one candle to create an atmosphere.
My cat is jumping up and down and around, and misses his head, oh dear!

Finally, getting down to business, his body is boiling with passion, and his
heart is set on fire; his kisses are deep with a tongue that doesn't tire.

He arrives bearing a present, the gift of his intoxicating manhood,
He never spends the night, a manage-a-trios with a cat is not good.

His love lives on inside me into the very next day,
It is late September, and today it feels like early May.

It feels as if Spring fever has arrived early, and just in the nick of time,
His kisses will last through the cold winter, a passion that all ends in rhyme.

The Jewish New Year has arrived with a blast from the ancient past,
Like an old teddy bear—the angel Gabriel is a passion that will last.

Sharon Esther Lampert
September 30, 2003

#1 Poetry Website for Student Projects

EL SHADDAI

"This poem is inspired by the fact that women are in charge of bringing life into the world and men are in charge of destroying life through war. We women knock them out and you guys knock them down."
Sharon Esther Lampert

Caressing my tender breasts,
his left hand's on the steering wheel,
and his right hand is firmly tucked
away inside my red silk dress.

He swerves the car to the curb
and turns off the ignition. Filling his
hungry mouth with my tasty tongue
- both hands caress my breasts -
Dangling keys dance to the Israeli music
playing on the radio, **"Chayal Shel Ahavah."**

Too old to be making love
in the front seat of his red van,
on a hot summer's night,
street lights on, glaring,
headlights off, flaring,
the moonlight beaming,
or am I dreaming?

Protruding, a bump below his
knee, a near-death experience:
the Israeli Army; inside Lebanon;
Sabra and Shatila; the fall; from
helicopter to hospital; an iron plate.
At home, fighting for his homeland,
a permanent dwelling; Iraqi parents
speaking Arabic, landed him on the
front lines of the bloody battlefield.
Jew, speak to your enemy in Arabic,
silently, with knives. A dangling gun
marches to military orders on the radio.

Me: sipping a pink Cosmo at Cibar;
red brick exterior and red velvet interior.
Him: toasting a **"L'Chaim"** with a Strawberry
Daiquiri. He speaks to me, **"Al-ha-ke-fak"**
and he is teaching me; and I look at him and
I look inside him:
an iron plate below his knee;
a locksmith for life;
a marriage gone sour;
an eviction after a lease expired;
an Orthodox Jew at a Chabad house;
his hands were full: **battle, blood, and bump, business and burden, bitch, Bible, and breast.**

Protruding, a engorged bump above
his knee, a near-life experience: an Israeli
man, an exotic accent, dark magnetic
eyes and chocolate-covered silk skin.
At home, in a temporary shelter, a sexy
exterior and a hot-blooded interior melted
me into his amorous arms. Melded together
as one, he speaks to his lover sweetly, **"Sing to me, Cha-mu-dah, of " Jerusalem of Gold," and of peace."**

Protrusions: an iron bump below his knee and
an engorged bump above his knee: a near-death
and a near-life experience: reaching again
for my ample breasts with loving hands and
a loving heart, suckling my pink nipples,
like a baby aching for his bottle of milk,
he speaks softly,
whispering into his lover's ear,
"I love your breasts."
I ask, "How do you say breasts in Hebrew?"
"Shadayim, Mo-tek, Shadayim."

Me: taking a spiritual detour, Shabbat at
the Chabad house, in a yellow dress that is
long enough to skim my knees, no protrusions,
only mystery. Illuminated is the fact that
in the Bible, the word Shaddai is God's name.
God speaks clearly with compassion:
God spoke to Moses and said to him:
"I am Yahweh. I appeared to Abraham, Isaac, and Jacob as El Shaddai."
Flickering Shabbat candles gleaming,
the moonlight beaming, or am I dreaming?
Shaddai provides a name of God that
celebrates the feminine attributes in God:
God: El Shaddai with shadayim—breasts.
Therefore, making perfect sense to me,
GOD IS A WOMAN. AL-HA-KE-FAK.

TRANSLATIONS
Hebrew: "Chayal shel Ahavah" is "Soldier of Love"
Hebrew: shadayim are breasts
Hebrew: "L'Chaim!" is " To Life!"
Arabic: "Al-ha-ke-fak" is "All is Excellent"
Hebrew: Cha-mu-dah is Darling
Hebrew: Motek is Sweetheart
"Jerusalem of Gold" is a famous song
Hebrew: Chabad house is a Jewish community center

Guidi Reni

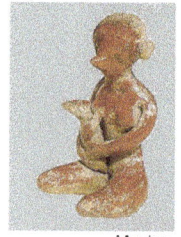
Gaugin

Mexico

Indian   Bangladesh   Stamp

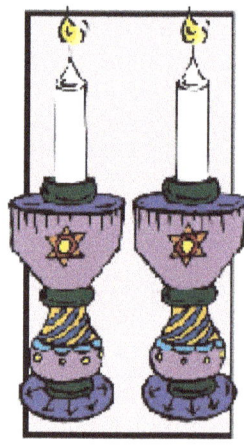

QUESTION
Is this poem a political, religious, or love poem?

REVIEWS
I love the way you weave together the erotic texture and spirtuality also.
This has such intense passion and faith. Thank you for sharing.
William Robbins

"A very thought provoking poem, Princess, that covers
a lot of ground, erotically, spiritually, and politically."
Robert D. Furrow

Map of Israel Illustration by Netta Wagner Shoshani

Sharon Esther Lampert
Sexiest Creative Genius in Human History
8th Prophetess of Israel: 22 Commandments
Special note of "Al-ha-ke-fak" to My Darling Muse, Roni.
© All Rights Reserved.

www.PoetryJewels.com
Diamonds, Emeralds, Sapphires, Rubies, and Pearls

THE SOLE INTENTION OF MY POETRY IS TO ADD LIGHT TO YOUR SOUL.

POETRY SEX SCANDAL AT BARNES & NOBLE

(YOUTUBE video)

BARNES & NOBLE
BOOKSELLERS

August 19, 2002

Sharon Esther Lampert
Kadimah Tribal Princess of Israel
P.O. Box 103
New York, NY 10028

Dear Sharon Esther Lampert:

Thanks for participating in our very successful monthly Open Mic hosted by Oreita Daley. Unfortunately, I have received complaints from customers attending the event regarding the erotica content of your poems, mentioning your commercial web site and passing out your poems and asking for audience participation.

The Open Mic is a program that was created to give as many poets as possible the opportunity to read and share their poetry with fellow poets and poetry lovers. Since the Open Mic takes place in a book store where customers are shopping, we ask the following:

Poets select material to read that is suitable for a general audience.

Poets be considerate of their fellow writers in choosing poems of appropriate length to read – so everyone has the opportunity to participate.

Poets should not pass out any kind of material including copies of poems or ask for audience participation.

Poets cannot promote their commercial web sites, products, services etc.

If you have any questions, please feel free to contact me directly.

Sincerely,

Frances Kelly
Frances Kelly
Community Relations Manager
Barnes & Noble
Upper E. Side (212) 794-2264

NYU Honored Sharon Esther Lampert with an Award for "Multi-Interdisciplinary Studies" (YOUTUBE video)

Poet
Prophet
Philosopher **Q**ueen
Peacemaker
Princess & **P**ea
PINUP
Performer
Player: Jock, NYU Varsity
Paladin of Education
PHOTON SUPERHERO
Princess Kadimah
8TH **P**rophetess of Israel
President
Publisher
Producer
Psychobiologist: Rockefeller U.
Piano-**P**laying Cat
Phoenix
Prodigy

My Websites:
SharonEstherLampert.com
PhilosopherQueen.com
WorldFamousPoems.com
PoetryJewels.com
GodIsGoDo.com
Schmaltzy.com
TrueLoveBurnsEternal.com
SillyLittleBoys.com
Smartgrades.com
EverydayanEasyA.com
PhotonSuperHero.com
BooksNotBombs.com
WritersRunTheWorld.com
PalmBeachBookPublisher.com
MiamiBookPublisher.com
HappyGrandparenting.com
BooksArePowerful.com
WinAtThin.com
WomenHaveAllThePower.com

SEE THE WORLD THROUGH THE EYES OF A CREATIVE GENIUS

About the Prodigy

SHARON ESTHER LAMPERT

V.E.S.S.E.L. Very. Extra. Special. Sharon. Esther. Lampert.

POET — One of the World's Greatest Poets "A LIST"
World Poetry Record: 120 Words of Rhyme from One Family of Rhyme
Greatest Poems Ever Written on Extraordinary World Events

http://famouspoetsandpoems.com/poets.html

PRODIGY

- Unleash the Creator, The God Within: 10 Esoteric Laws of Genius and Creativity

PROPHET— GOD IS GO! DO!

- The 22 Commandments: All You Will Ever Need to Know About God
- God Talks to Me: A Working Definition of God

PHILOSOPHER QUEEN

- Temporary Insanity: We Are All Building Our Lives on a Sand Trap—Written in Letter S
- God of What? Is Life a Gift or a Punishment? 10 Absolute Truths
- WOMEN HAVE ALL THE POWER But They Never Learned How to Use It!
- Sperm Manifesto: 10 Rules for the Road

PEACEMAKER

World Peace Equation.com

PHOTON SUPERHERO OF EDUCATION

PALADIN OF EDUCATION

SMARTGRADES BRAIN POWER REVOLUTION
- "The Silent Crisis Destroying America's Brightest Minds"

BOOK OF THE MONTH, Alma Public Library, Wisconsin
- EVERYDAY AN EASY A.com
- 40 Universal Gold Standards of Education
- Intra-personal Integration Therapy
- 15 Stepping Stones of Academic Successs
- 15 Stumbling Blocks of Academic Failure

Pioneer

- SILLY LITTLE BOYS: 40 Rules of Manhood
- LYMTY: Love You More Than Yesterday
  14 Relationship Strategies for Happily Ever After
- In One Hour, Read Hebrew
- CUPID: The Language of Love — Written in Letter C
- PUBLISH: The Secret Sauce of Book Sales — Written in Letter P
- Win at Thin: Fat Me, Skinny Me — Written in Letter A

PIN-UP

SEXIEST CREATIVE GENIUS IN HUMAN HISTORY

Artists March to the Beat of a Different Drummer
Sharon Esther Lampert Marches to the Beat of an Entire Orchestra

Poet, Philosopher, Prophet
Paladin of Education, Peacemaker
Princess & Pea, Phoenix, PHOTON, PINUP, Prodigy

Big-Blue-Eyes. Brilliant Books. Beautiful & Buxom. Blessed.

Sharon Esther Lampert was born an **OLD SOUL** — She was never young! Sharon is a lefty.
At age nine, her mother declared: **"My daughter is a poet, philosopher, and teacher!"**
At age nine, Sharon was writing books on memo pads, and binding them together with a stapler.
When Sharon walked into a room, her mother would proclaim, **"THE QUEEN HAS ARRIVED!"**

Her mother nicknamed her daughter, **"The Princess and the Pea!"** Sharon's greatest literary works woke her up in the middle of the night — and made her get up out of bed — and write them down. Sharon writes an entire book in one night! eg., GOD TALKS TO ME: A WORKING DEFINITION OF GOD

Sharon's literary genius is to amalgamate poetry, philosophy, and comedy into one sentence.
Sharon's BIG BRAIN conceptualizes BIG IDEAS using one letter of the alphabet: C, S, D and P.
Sharon's mother was the sole person in Sharon's life who knew who Sharon was from the **INSIDE OUT!**

Her beloved mother also knew to her very last breath... the exact day and to-the minute when she would die! (Eve Paikoff Lampert: June 3, 1925 — May 5, 1985).

Sharon Esther's Gifts Are Metaphysical — Beyond the Scope of Scientific Inquiry

There Are No Rough Drafts! — My Books Write Themselves!
(There Are 4 Books with God in the Title)

"A LIST" Sharon Esther Lampert is One of the World's Greatest Poets
http://famouspoetsandpoems.com/poets.html

#1 Poetry Website for Student Projects

On a global scale, Sharon's poetry is used by teachers for their poetry lesson plans, and by students for their poetry projects.

New York University Awards (YOUTUBE Videos) BA, MA, MA

Sharon Esther earned three degrees from NYU — and she was honored with two NYU awards.
Sharon represented her class at her M.A. graduation — and was honored with an award for **"Multi-Interdisciplinary Studies."**
She also played on the NYU Women's Varsity Basketball Team as a Center in the $16-million Coles Sports Center.
Sharon won an "NYU Weightlifting Contest"— Sharon was the sole contestant—so she won! (NYU Washington Square News article).

"When I'm not writing, I'm reading. When I'm not writing or reading, I'm singing." (YOUTUBE videos).
—Sharon Esther Lampert

One of the World's Greatest Poets

http://famouspoetsandpoems.com/poets.html

List of Poets - Famous Poets and Poems   http://famouspoetsandpoems.com/poets.html

 Larry Levis (3) (1946 - 1996)

 Amy Levy (69) (1861 - 1889)

 Louise Labe (1) (1524 - 1566)

 David Lehman (58) (1948 - present)

 Jiri Mordecai Langer (1) (1894 - 1943)

 John Lindley (4) (1952 - present)

 Dimitris Lyacos (3) (1966 - present)

 Yahia Lababidi (10) (1973 - present)

 Laurie Lee (6) (1914 - 1997)

 Walter Savage Landor (52) (1775 - 1864)

 Michael Lally (1) (1942 - present)

 Major Henry Livingston, Jr. (23) (1748 - 1828)

 Roddy Lumsden (2) (1966 - present)

 Sharmagne Leland-St. John (5) (1953 - present)

 Sharon Esther Lampert (19) (0 - present)

M

 Claude McKay (76) (1889 - 1948)

 Spike Milligan (35) (1918 - 2002)

 Marianne Moore (18) (1887 - 1972)

 John Milton (102) (1608 - 1674)

 A. A. Milne (22) (1882 - 1956)

 Czeslaw Milosz (33) (1911 - 2004)

 Edgar Lee Masters (251) (1868 - 1950)

 William Matthews (10) (1942 - 1997)

 Edwin Muir (14) (1887 - 1959)

 Roger McGough (14) (1937 - present)

 Walter de la Mare (44) (1873 - 1956)

 Antonio Machado (8) (1875 - 1939)

 Edna St. Vincent Millay (165) (1892 - 1950)

 W. S. Merwin (23) (1927 - present)

 John Masefield (25) (1878 - 1967)

 Louis MacNeice (3) (1907 - 1963)

 Thomas Moore (144) (1779 - 1852)

 Christopher Marlowe (6) (1564 - 1593)

What Happens When You Dress Up Albert Einstein As Marilyn Monroe?
SHARON ESTHER LAMPERT

SEE THE WORLD THROUGH THE EYES OF A CREATIVE GENIUS

FAN MAIL
FANS@SharonEstherLampert.com

FAN MAIL
FANS@SharonEstherLampert.com

A PHENOMENON...
SHARON ESTHER LAMPERT

Lithe and lovely ... like a fawn.
This lady fascinates me ... from dusk till dawn.
Feminine and comely ... she's beyond belief
A blue-beam from her eyes ... is my soothing relief.

Girlish in her braces ... maidenly in her style
I yearn for her embraces ... and adore her friendly smile.
As tasteful as any artist ... you'll ever see
She's a compendium of class ... from A to Z.

If you'd like to see a figure, that puts Venus to shame
Behold her in a swimsuit, and your passions will aflame.
Ever exuding goodness . . . guided from above
Miss Sharon is the essence, and epitome of Love.

She's the inspiration of sages, and also fools like me
And the most magnificent female, I'm sure I'll ever see.
The nights are now endearing, & never filled with doubt
I sometimes wake up singing, cause it's Sharon . . .
I dream about.

Affectionately,. .
A devoted fan,
Harry McVeety

FAN MAIL
FANS@SharonEstherLampert.com

Dear Sharon,

You are not only an exquisite poet, you're beautiful! Am smitten by your luminous beingness. Are you an angel in disguise--a so-called malachim in Hebrew if I am not mistaken.

Thank you for your wondeful open-hearted response.

Your photo will sit next to those of Gautama Buddha and the Blessed Virgin Mary.

I will follow your sound esoteric advise regarding the positioning of your photo and the two other icons.

I am deeply impressed that you are very conscious about the concept of sacred space and the flow of spiritual energy.

So please send me your precious photo as soon as possible.

P.S. Will you be generous enough to send me your signed photo which I will place on the secret altar of my heart, lit by the menorah, the seven-stemmed candelabra of your inspiration, O mystical muse, O Rose of Sharon...

Your ardent fan and admirer,

Felix Fojas, the cybercat with a mystical meow
Chico, CA, 95926

FAN MAIL
FANS@SharonEstherLampert.com

Congregation Emanu-El
of the City of New York
Fifth Avenue at Sixty-fifth Street
New York, N.Y. 10021-6596

Study of
DAVID M. POSNER

September 22, 1999

The New York Public Library
Humanities and Social Sciences Library
Fifth Avenue and 42nd Street
New York, NY 10018-2788

Dear Friends:

Sharon Esther Lampert has made application for a fellowship from the Center for Scholars and Writers. It is with greatest pleasure that I write to you in support of her application.

I can best describe this remarkable woman by citing the analysis of Moses Maimonides, in his "Guide for the Perplexed," concerning psychological endowments. He noted the class of people who are intellectually superior, but whose imaginative faculties are deficient. These, he said, were philosophers. Then there are those whose imaginative faculties are highly developed, but who are deficient intellectually. He said these are dreamers and politicians. But then he observed the rare people who have both highly developed intellects and imaginations. These, he said, are prophets.

Sharon Esther Lampert falls into the last category. She has one of the most gifted intellects I have ever encountered, and her imaginative capacity is absolutely awesome.

I have known many people throughout my long career at Temple Emanu-El. I have never met anyone like this extraordinary human being.

Again, awesome is the most appropriate word.

Yours truly,

[signature]

FORMED BY THE CONSOLIDATION OF EMANU-EL CONGREGATION AND TEMPLE BETH-EL

#1 Poetry Website
for Student Projects

FAN MAIL
FANS@SharonEstherLampert.com

Windsor High School
6208 Hwy 61-67
Imperial, Mo 63052

Sharon Esther Lampert
P.O.BOX 103,
New York, New York, 10028, US

Cody Howell
1042 Prospect Dr.
Imperial, Mo 63052
May 2, 2005

Sharon Esther Lampert
P.O.BOX 103,
New York, New York,10028,US

Dear, Sharon E. Lampert

Hello, My name in Cody, I am a Junior at Windsor High School in Missouri. I have had the chance to write to any one person and I picked you. I have always enjoyed quotes and sayings. Theirs just something about it, like I have always known there is a "better way" but never really found anything until I started to pay attention that their was more than just physical happenings. The poet has the ability to drink from streams science has yet to discover. I used to always reads one liners like
" a community begins to grow when old men plant trees they know they will never enjoy the shade of." Things like this really interested me. Something more than what I had known.

I am very curious by nature, and this kind of wisdom/intellect really hit the spot for me, now I have many poems, sayings, quotes ext. I can't recite them by heart but I thourouly enjoyed the ones I read. I didn't know of you until me and my buddy were talking about how we like psychology and basically more than average and the "better way". After reading some of your quotes I realized you must have seen your share of happenings and become very wise over the years of thought, poetry, and life.

My first thought was to write to you and try to flatter you because I enjoyed your work. Well I guess you made your poetry your work. Then I started thinking that this well of knowledge , all that stuff you've learned, it would be a long shot but my curiosity wouldn't stop unless if I asked you if you could share some of the knowledge you have gained. Any and all would be appreciated and probably useful later considering I am still just a 17-year-old kid. I can't think of any other word than greedy, but you have already thought so many with your influences, and I ask you to help me out, If your busy you have already done more than enough, thank you, and thanks for your time while reading this. I am sorry but I always find myself looking for more and I'm positive you have gained useful info in your day. I could imagine the child who has heard many stories, lesions, and wisdoms of many. He'd be one of the most diverse ,intelligent humans around, and with something like this in mind how could I not be greedy.

I have already learned some from Internet, friends like the one who told me about poems, and family. I have tried to learn patience from the impatient, kindness from the angry, and truth from fools, but for some reason I'm not thankful for these teachers. I still feel as if I could have more, and the lessons of an older experienced poet just has something about how it sounds. Greatness is all I've seen come from poets their ability to make one think is amazing , I could just imagine the wisdom of an experienced one.

Either way I just wanted to say thank you for your time and thank you for doing what you have done. Your shared wisdom and lessons will help many and your work might not be remembered forever but I believe that your positive effect will. Thank you again

Your student ,
Cody

Date: Thursday, November 19, 2009, 3:11 PM

Dear Ms. Lampert,
I am working on a poetry project for my senior English class. Instead of a boring research paper we are to analyze a famous poet and make a power point, and a creative presentation over the poets life, work and also criticisms of their work. The last part is the problem, I can't seem to find any scholarly criticisms of your work. Do you know of any, or have on record any criticisms of your work, either oral or written? My project partner and I would love to do our project on you because we find you very interesting and your poems very in tune with the lives of people today and the problems we face as modern people. Any help would be appreciated.
Thank you again.
Sincerely,
—Michael Rockey

Date: April 10, 2009 6:15:32 PM

Hi Sharon!
My name is Alexa & I'm a junior in high school! I love your poems, especially about world affairs. I will be doing a poetry analysis on three of your poems **(I've chosen Sandstorm in Iraq, Tsunami, and There Is No Flower in Darfur)** and also a presentation to inform the class of your works, accomplishments & biography. I have been searching every website and library on some information about you, but can't find any! If you can it would be greatly appreciated if you could tell me a little about your childhood, parents, education, religious beliefs, and maybe some experiences that have shaped your views or positions in regards to your poetry!
Thanks so much!
Have an amazing day!
—Alexa Young

Date: January 20, 2010 9:54:04 PM

Hello Miss Lampert,
My name is Kal Marshall, I am a student at Johnson City High School, Johnson City, New York. I am currently enrolled in AP English and Literature. My teacher realized my classes misunderstanding for poetry and decided to have us write paper on a poem of our choice and about the poet. While searching the web for an interesting poem I came among yours and knew it was the poem I was meant to write a paper on. One part of the paper is to "Interview" someone who has read the poem. While I was on your website I found the little note about E-mailing you. So I was wondering if you would be willing to give me a little more detail on your poem, **"EDUCATE NOT."** From the basis under which it was derived from, to your true feeling and understanding of the poem, to how you feel about it now from when you were writing it. Your Bio is extremely interesting, and I hope to learn more. Thank you very much for creating a poem I could actually enjoy to spend a month working on. and hopefully I hear back from you in a reasonable time.
Thanks Again,
—Kal Marshall

Gazillions...
National & International Poetry Publications

Afghanistan: RAHA
2003:
Princess Kadimah is Published in Afghanistan: RAHA
Dear Sharon
I added you to my list and also your work is published on the net:
http://rahapen.org/options_poetry_Sharon.htm
Regards
—Kamran Mirhazar
Raha PEN Club
Email: rahapen@kabulpress.org
0093-799390025
Kabul, Afghanistan: Post Box number: 3219

Dear Sharon Esther Lampert,
Your artistic poem CENTRAL PARK: Water Fight, Flight and Tears marked by true creative genius,
has been published in the June of Taj Mahal Review an International Literary Journal ISSN 0972-6004.
This Journal contains 300 pages of short stories, literary articles and poems by authors from all over the world.
The Journal is an attempt to select the best of world poetry.
Best Wishes
—RADHA AGRAWAL
www.cyberwit.net
4/2 B, L.I.G.
Govindpur Colony Allahabad - 211004 (U.P.)
INDIA

Dear Sharon,
When we made our recent call for submissions, in which we asked for writings pertaining to the terrorist attacks of September 11, 2001, we were unsure what kind of response we would get. As it turns out, we have received poetry, fiction, and essays from writers all over the world. Our "feature writer section" for October will include the work of over 100 writers. We are very happy to include your work in this section. Your contribution to this project is an integral part of the overall tone and spirit of the October issue. We want to thank you for helping us in this project and, more importantly, expressing yourself at a time when to do so is both difficult and essential. Thank you again for sending us your work.
The October issue will come out on October 21, 2001.
 Sincerely,
 The Pedestal Magazine
 www.thepedestalmagazine.com

Sharon, Thanks for the note. I really appreciate it. A gift, huh? Wow, I am intigued and flattered. By the way, several people really liked your writing in the current Pedestal.
Best,
—John Amen

Gazillions...
National & International Poetry Publications

Dear Sharon,
Thank you so much for the kind comments.
I am pleased to have your poems Timeless Sandcastles and Sacred Feathers Of Divine Freedoms appearing in the first issue of Thought Fragments.
I will send you a reminder email when the first issue goes up.
Once again, thank you.
Best wishes,
—Darlene Zagata

Featured Poem of the Month:
Cool...thanks!
It's a pleasure to feature your work.
I want you to know that i have a lot of respect and admiration for Jewish people.
I look forward to learning more about you and your culture through your work.
—Nate

Dear Sharon,
Several weeks ago we informed you by mail that our editors wish to include your poetry in a new collection of poems written by the Best poets we have encountered. We need to hear back from you immediately if you wish to be included in the special edition . . .
The Best Poems and Poets of 2002
Library of Congress ISBN 0-7951-5175-6

Dear Sharon,
My name is August Highland - i am a writer and editor - i read your work
i dream forge - i like your work - a lot - i want to include your work in the next issue of the little literary -journal of which i am the editor - you can see the muse apprentice guild at www.muse-apprentice-guild.com - internet explorer 5.5 or higher is required send me as many pieces as you like sharon and they can be of any
length - also include a short bio
Always,
—August

Dear Sharon,
We have discussed this at length and have concluded that your
poems are truly unique and rather exciting.
Fondly,
—Ruby M.
Editor, PrinsessTarta Magazine

Sharon,
How do we get your poem into my site?
—Richard Williams, Editor

WORLD FAMOUS QUOTES

THERE IS ONE GLOBAL ENEMY: IGNORANCE
—PHOTON SUPERHERO OF EDUCATION

LONELINESS IS DEATH
SOLITUDE IS DIVINE
—Philosopher Queen Sharon Esther Lampert

BE HARD
ON A WOMAN ONLY WHEN MAKING LOVE TO HER
—Philosopher Queen Sharon Esther Lampert

FIGHT TO LIVE
LIVE TO FIGHT
BORN TO DIE
—Philosopher Queen Sharon Esther Lampert

THERE IS ONLY ONE
TRUTH
NO ONE HAS THE TRUTH
—Philosopher Queen Sharon Esther Lampert

WORLD FAMOUS QUOTES

It's Not Easy Being a Jewish Sex Symbol But Someone Has to Do It!

— Prodigy Sharon Esther Lampert

THE 11 COMMANDMENT
KEEP THEM LAUGHING KEEP THEM SANE

There Are 5 Books of Moses and 5000 Books of Jewish Comedy

—Princess Kadimah, 8TH Prophetess of Israel

GOD IS GO! DO!

God Can Only Do for You, What God Can Do Through You

God is Not Physics — The Laws of the Universe
God is Metaphysics — Beyond the Scope of Scientific Inquiry
Like Mind, Thoughts, and Ideas — Beyond the Scope of Scientific Inquiry

—Prophet Sharon Esther Lampert

Less Than 1% of Population and 22% of Nobel Prizes

Wherever Jews Go, Grass Grows
Wherever Israelis Go, Gardens Grow

—Princess Kadimah, 8TH Prophetess of Israel

KADIMAH PRESS: Gifts of Genius

18 BOOKS OF POETRY
Poet: The Greatest Poems Ever Written on Extraordinary World Events
Title: I Stole All the Words from the Dictionary
#1 Poetry Website for School Projects
A List: One of the World's Greatest Poets
ISBN Hardcover: 978-1-885872-06-7
ISBN Paperback: 978-1-885872-07-4
ISBN E-Book: 978-1-885872-08-1

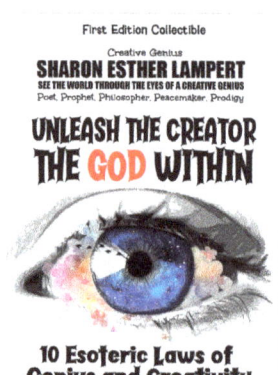

Prodigy: WORLD PREMIERE!
Title: Unleash the Creator The God Within
10 Esoteric Laws of Genius and Creativity
ISBN Hardcover: 978-1-885872-21-0
ISBN Paperback: 978-1-885872-22-7
ISBN E-Book: 978-1-885872-23-4

Prophet: WORLD PREMIERE! GOD IS GO! DO!
Title: GOD TALKS TO ME: A WORKING DEFINITION OF GOD
ISBN Hardcover: 978-1-885872-33-3
ISBN Paperback: 978-1-885872-34-0
ISBN E-Book: 978-1-885872-36-4

Prophet: WORLD PREMIERE!
Title: The 22 Commandments: All You Will Ever Need to Know About God
A Universal Moral Compass For All People, For All Religions, For All Time
ISBN Hardcover: 978-1-885872-03-6
ISBN Paperback: 978-1-885872-04-3
ISBN E-Book: 978-1-885872-05-0

Philosopher: WORLD PREMIERE!
Title: God of What? Is Life a Gift or a Punishment? 10 Absolute Truths
ISBN Hardcover: 978-1-885872-00-5
ISBN Paperback: 978-1-885872-01-2
ISBN E-Book: 978-1-885872-02-9
GodofWhat.com

KADIMAH PRESS: *Gifts of Genius*

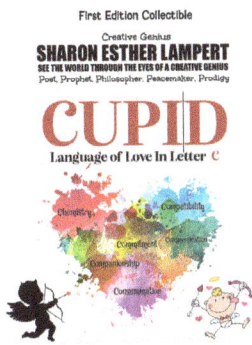

Prodigy: WORLD PREMIERE!
Title: CUPID: The Language of Love—Written in Letter C
ISBN Hardcover: 978-1-885872-55-5
ISBN Paperback: 978-1-885872-56-2
ISBN E-Book: 978-1-885872-57-9
SharonEstherLampert.com

Prodigy: WORLD PREMIERE!
Title: TEMPORARY INSANITY
We Are All Building Our Lives on a Sand Trap — Written in Letter S
ISBN Hardcover: 978-1-885872-70-8
ISBN E-Book: 978-1-885872-71-5
SharonEstherLampert.com

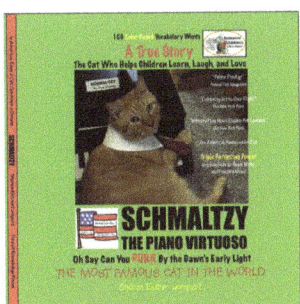

Popular: Children's Book, Ages 8-12
Title: SCHMALTZY: IN AMERICA, EVEN A CAT CAN HAVE A DREAM
ISBN Hardcover: 978-1-885872-39-5
ISBN Paperback: 978-1-885872-38-8
ISBN E-Book: 978-1-885872-37-1
Schmaltzy.com

Color-Coded Vocabulary Words

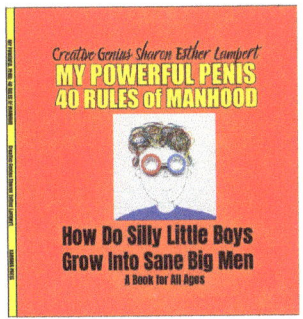

Popular: WORLD PREMIERE
Title: 40 RULES OF MANHOOD
HOW DO SILLY LITTLE BOYS GROW INTO SANE BIG MEN
14 Global Catastrophes of Violence Against Women
ISBN Hardcover: 978-1-885872-29-6
ISBN Paperback: 978-1-885872-35-7
ISBN E-Book: 978-1-885872-41-8
SillyLittleBoys.com

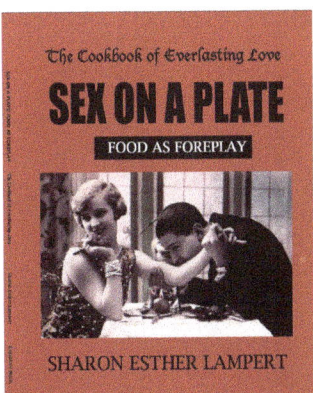

Popular: Every Relationship Begins with a Great Meal
Title: SEX ON A PLATE: FOOD AS FOREPLAY
THE COOKBOOK OF EVERLASTING LOVE
ISBN Hardcover: 978-1-885872-46-3
ISBN Paperback: 978-1-885872-48-7
ISBN E-Book: 978-1-885872-47-0
TrueLoveBurnsEternal.com

Count Your Blessings. Practice Gratitude

"Never Underestimate the Power of a Girl with a Book"
—ICON Supreme-Court Justice Ruth Bader Ginsburg

1. MY GENETIC GIFT OF GENIUS
- Lefty: Born with an Extra Body Part, "Creative Apparatus"
- Two Sets of Artsy-Fartsy Genes: Maternal Grandfather Benjamin Paikoff and Father Abraham Lampert
- Vocalist: Ashira Orchestra (YOUTUBE videos)
- Athlete: NYU Women's Varsity Basketball Team

2. MY LIFE: Dawn of Digital Revolution
- The Golden Age of Personal Computers: APPLE
- The Golden Age of Creativity: ADOBE
- The Golden Age of Email, Internet, and Globalization

NYU President Andrew Hamilton and Me

NYU Special Mention
NYU President John Brademas (backed his limosine into my bicycle)
Professor Yael Feldman (the writer's relationship to MOMMY)
Professor Paul Humphreys (class on family therapy)
Professor Ted Coons, (my position at Rockefeller University)
John, The Security Guard at Coles Sports Center (SUPERFAN)
NYU B-Ball Coaches: Evelyn Hannon and Sherri Pickard

3. MY LOVED ONES:
- UNCONDITIONAL TRUE LOVE: MOMMY
- My PURRfect Children: SCHMALTZY & FALAFEL, Schmaltzy.com (YOUTUBE videos)
- My Muse: NYU Professor Karl Bardosh "Friends First and Forever and Family"
- My Metaphysical Sister: Poet Hannah Szenes: "ELI, ELI"

4. MY EDUCATION: BA, MA, MA. and Awards (YOUTUBE videos)
- NYU MENTOR Laurin Raiken: NYU **"Multi-Interdisciplinary Award"** and **M.A. Class Representative**
- NY ROCKEFELLER UNIVERSITY, Publication: "Hyperphagia and Obesity Induced by Neuropeptide Y"
- 100-Year Scholarship Award Winner, Presented by NYC Mayor Edward Koch
- Empire Science Scholarship Award Winner
- First Prize: Upper East Side Writing Contest
- Jerusalem Fellowship Award of Aish Hatorah, ISRAEL
- Won a Weightlifting Contest, NYU Coles Sports Center (Washington Square News)

5. MY SPORTS:
- NYC Marathon
- Basketball: NYU Women's Varsity Basketball Team, Center
- Basketball: NYC Urban Professional League
- Skiing: Heavenly, Lake Tahoe, Nevada
- Tennis: Central Park Tennis Courts
- Basketball and Baseball — Coach Sandy Pyonin
- Baseball: Hall of Fame Jean Harding and Wilma Briggs

NYU Professor Karl Bardosh and Me

6. MY INSPIRATIONS:
- ISRAEL: "AM YISRAEL CHAI!" Sheep to Slaughter to Light of the World!
- Rabbi David Posner, Temple Emanu-El NYC, "President of My Fan Club"
- NYC: Personal Freedom and Creative Freedom
- America: Land of Unlimited Possibility

NYU Professor Laurin Raiken and Me

South Florida Sun-Sentinel

DELRAY BEACH NEWS   PALM BEACH COUNTY NEWS

Spirituality workshop supports A Walk on Water fund

MARCI SHATZMAN MSHATZMAN@TRIBPUB.COM | JAN 20, 2016

Sharon Esther Lampert didn't bring her tiara when she moved here from New York, but she found one just in time to be one of the speakers at Barbara M. Wolk's second annual Spirituality Workshop Jan. 24.

"Barbara has this wonderful event in support of autistic children," said Lampert, an author, poet, philosopher and educator who plays a princess for her talks.

She expects to hand out her "30 Commandments: All You Ever Need to Know," at the workshop from 10:30 a.m. to 12:30 p.m. at the Shirley & Barton Weisman Community Center, 7091 W. Atlantic Ave., in Delray Beach.

Admission is a minimum of $10 and the event opens at 10 a.m. A live auction will include a sculpture called "Balance."

EVERY THOUGHT IN YOUR HEAD WAS PUT THERE BY A WRITER
— Sharon Esther Lampert

I Am **M**ortal.
My Books Are **I**mmortal.
Please Handle My Books Gently.
My Books Are My Remains.

This book was compiled in three parts.
Part 1. Birth—Age 9-Present
Part 2. Format Book—June 11-25, 2022
Part 3. Publish—August 18, 2022

Sharon Esther Lampert
SEE THE WORLD THROUGH THE EYES OF A CREATIVE GENIUS
Poet, **P**rophet, **P**hilosopher, **P**eacemaker, **P**rincess & **P**ea, **P**rodigy

FAIR USE NOTICE

There are a few copyrighted materials whose use has not been specifically authorized by the copyright owner. We are making this material available in its efforts to advance the understanding of poetry, philosophy, spirituality, and education. We believe this constitutes a 'fair use' of the copyrighted material as provided for in Section 107 of the US Copyright Law.